Bahama Mama's Cooking

140 AUTHENTIC RECIPES FROM THE BEAUTIFUL
TROPICAL ISLANDS OF THE BAHAMAS.
APPETIZERS, DRINKS, BREAKFASTS, SEAFOOD, CHICKEN,
PORK, BEEF, DESSERTS AND MORE

Publisher/Editor .... Capt. Jan Robinson
Associate Editor .... Barbara Lawrence
Production .... Gracie Martin
Proofreader .... Fernand Dionne
Interior Illustrations. .... Image Club Graphics, Inc.
Cover Watercolor Painting .... Pat Anderson

www.SHIPTOSHOREINC.com

SHIP TO SHORE, INC

10500 Mount Holly Road • Charlotte • NC • 28214
Phone 704-394-2433 • 704-392-4777 Fax
email: CapJan@aol.com
www.SHIPTOSHOREINC.com
P.O. Box 10898 • St. Thomas • USVI • 00801
Phone/Fax 340-775-6295

To order additional copies or for a *free* catalog
1-800-338-6072
www.SHIPTOSHOREINC.com
email CapJan@aol.com

BAHAMA MAMA'S COOKING

Library of Congress card catalog number 93-926-36
Bahama Mama's Cooking: 140 authentic Bahamian recipes; Jan Robinson
Includes index
1. Cookery, Caribbean   I. Title

Printed in the United States of America
First Printing: May, 1996
Second Printing: May. 1998
Third Printing: May, 2001

ISBN 0-9612686-7-0

ACKNOWLEDGEMENTS

My sincerest thanks and warmest appreciation to all of my wonderful friends throughout the Caribbean and especially to those on the islands of the Bahamas, who have shared delicious meals and special times with me throughout the years. Thank you for sharing your treasured recipes. It is because of you that many will share these heartwarming dishes.

Also, many thanks to Janet Maury McLean for her recipe files and Bahamian knowledge, Vicky Northmore, Mary Ellen Krell, Barbara Lawrence, and Shelle Kelly (my goddaughter, now married, living in Nassau, where she tends her store "Island Tings" on Bay Street).

Many thanks for testing, tasting, and proofreading the recipes as we adapted them for **Bahama Mama's Cooking**.

FOREWORD

Bahama Mama's Cooking is as inviting as the beautiful islands and people which inspired it. Consisting of more than 700 islands and about 2,000 cays, the nation of the Bahamas is spread out over 100,000 square miles of the Atlantic Ocean with some islands located as close as 50 miles east of Florida.

The islands are mostly flat and the soil is shallow and rocky, yet wonderfully fertile. For hundreds of years, Bahamians have grown many exotic fruits and vegetables. The sea harvest of the Bahamas abounds with conch, crayfish, crab, rock lobster, hog snapper, grouper, yellow tail and whelk.

On his first trip to the New World in 1492, Christopher Columbus landed on one of the islands– although historians still dispute which island. Columbus was astonished by the sea life and recorded its wonder in his log book. *"There are fish here so unlike ours, that it is a marvel. No man would not wonder at them or be anything but delighted to see them."*

Today, the Bahamas is a popular tourist destination with travelers from North and South America, Europe and the Far East. And, with the recent explosion of cruise ship and charter yacht traffic, Bahamian cuisine is being tasted and appreciated by an ever-increasing number of visitors.

Traditional Bahamian cooking is imaginative and creative, following a "make do with what you've got" cooking style. **Bahama Mama's Cooking** offers something to suit all tastes. There are wonderful blends of spices in these delicious breads, vegetarian meals, side dishes, salads, appetizers, meats, beverages, soups and desserts. And, they are simple to prepare.

Bahama Mama's Cooking is the first in a new series of cookbooks from *Ship To Shore Inc.* featuring exotic and traditional recipes from tropical islands. As we continue to promote the cooking of the islands, it is our hope that we will share with you the joy and good times that went into the preparation of these meals. Bon Appetit!

BAHAMA MAMA'S
Cooking

TABLE OF CONTENTS

ABOUT THE AUTHOR

Capt. Jan Robinson (The Galley Gourmet™) is a native of New Zealand; she divides her time between residences in the U.S. Virgin Islands and North Carolina. Jan loves to travel exploring other cuisines, particularly those of the Islands. *Bahama Mama's Cooking* is the seventh volume in her popular *Ship to Shore Cookbook Series*. Robinson is an accredited member of the American Institute of Wine and Food and holds certificates from the Cordon Bleu Cooking School, the Ritz Cooking School, the Culinary Institute of America, and a U.S. Coast Guard captain's license.

Robinson's television cooking credits include "The Morning Show" with Regis Philbin and the NBC special "The Cruise of the Vanity," which featured Jan and her yacht. As "The Galley Gourmet™" Robinson authors *Southern Boating Magazine's* monthly column "At Ease in the Galley" and a monthly column for *All At Sea* an international monthly. She has also been profiled in numerous national and international publications and is a much sought-after host and judge of cooking competitions.

Visit our website
www.SHIPTOSHOREINC.com

Bahama Mama's Breads

PINEAPPLE MANGO BREAD

PREPARATION TIME: 15 MINUTES
COOKING TIME: 40 MINUTES
SERVES: 6 - 8

2 cups flour
1-1/4 cups granulated sugar
1/2 tsp. salt
2 tsp. cinnamon
2 tsp. baking soda
3/4 cup vegetable oil
3 eggs
1 can (6 oz.) crushed pineapple
2 cups chopped mango
1/2 cup chopped pecans or walnuts

Preheat oven to 350°F. Sift together all dry ingredients in a large bowl.
Mix well and add oil, eggs, pineapple. Beat well. Add mango and nuts.
Pour into a well-greased and floured loaf pan. Bake 40 minutes.

Banana Muffins

PREPARATION TIME: 10 MINUTES
COOKING TIME: 20-25 MINUTES
SERVES: 12

3/4 cup granulated sugar
1/2 cup butter
1 egg, beaten
1-1/4 cups mashed bananas
1/2 tsp. vanilla
1 tsp. baking soda, dissolved in 1 Tblsp. hot water
1-1/2 cups flour

Preheat oven to 350°F. Mix sugar, butter, egg, bananas, vanilla and baking soda until creamy. Add the flour. Do not overmix. Bake 20-25 minutes until golden brown and toothpick comes out clean.

Coconut Bread

PREPARATION TIME: 15 MINUTES
COOKING TIME: 1 HOUR
SERVES: 10 - 12

1 cup shredded coconut
4 cups flour
2 cups sugar
1 tsp. cinnamon
1 tsp. nutmeg
2 tsp. vanilla
2 tsp. baking powder
1 cup milk
1/2 cup cream of coconut (Coco Lopez)
4 Tblsp. sour cream
1 tsp. salt
4 eggs, beaten

Preheat oven to 350°F. Mix all ingredients (mixture will be thick). Separate into two 5 x 9 inch greased loaf pans. Bake 1 hour or until done. Remove from pans and cool on racks.

Serve warm with butter as an accompaniment to chowder or soup and a cheese board. Great as a cocktail snack when spread with cream cheese.

JOHNNY CAKES

PREPARATION TIME: 10 MINUTES
COOKING TIME: 30-35 MINUTES
YIELD: 6 - 9 DUMPLINGS

1 cup all-purpose flour
1-1/2 tsp. baking powder
1/2 tsp. salt
1 Tblsp. butter
Water
1/4 cup vegetable oil

Sift the flour, baking powder, and salt into a bowl. Cut in the butter. Slowly add enough cold water to make a stiff dough. Knead on a lightly floured board until smooth. Shape into small balls, about the size of a large golf ball and flatten in the palm of your hand.

Heat the vegetable oil in a skillet, add the dumplings and cook until golden brown on both sides. *Serve warm.*

Hint: *For a tasty variation, add 1 whole skinned chile pepper, diced small, after you have mixed the dry ingredients together.*

Note: For a thicker consistency use 2/3 cup flour and 1/3 cup cornmeal.

Pepper Cheese Bread

PREPARATION TIME: 10 MINUTES
COOKING TIME: 1 HOUR
SERVES: 4

1 cup cream style corn
1 cup yellow corn meal
1 tsp. baking soda
3/4 cup milk
1/4 cup vegetable oil
1 cup grated cheddar cheese
2 cans (3 oz.) whole green chile peppers

Preheat oven to 350° F. Combine ingredients. Pour some of the batter into a 9 x 13 inch pan. Layer with cheddar cheese and whole green chiles. Repeat, finishing with cheese and chiles. Bake 1 hour or until cooked.

Mama's Easy Muffins

PREPARATION TIME: 10 MINUTES
COOKING TIME: 20 MINUTES
SERVES: 4 - 6

1 pint vanilla ice cream, softened
2 cups sifted self-rising flour

Preheat oven to 350°F. Blend ice cream and flour until flour is just moistened (batter will be lumpy). Fill 10 well greased muffin cups 3/4 full. Bake 20 minutes or until toothpick comes out dry.

Note: *Any flavor ice cream will work. Try your favorite flavors for tasty variations.*

Mama's Best Gingerbread

PREPARATION TIME: 20 MINUTES
COOKING TIME: 45 MINUTES
SERVES: 12

1/2 cup softened butter
1/2 cup granulated sugar
1 egg, beaten
2-1/2 cups flour, sifted
1-1/2 tsp. baking soda
1 tsp. cinnamon
1 tsp. ginger
1/2 tsp. cloves
1/2 tsp. salt
1 cup molasses
1 cup hot water

Preheat oven to 350°F. Cream butter and sugar. Add eggs. Sift together all dry ingredients. Combine molasses and hot water. Add dry ingredients to butter and sugar alternately with liquid, a small amount at a time. Beat after each addition until smooth. Bake in a greased and floured 9 x 9 x 2 inch pan 45 minutes or until inserted toothpick comes out clean.

Pumpkin Bread

Preparation time: 20 minutes
Cooking time: 50 minutes
Serves: 12

2/3 cup softened butter
2-2/3 cups sugar
4 eggs
2 cups cooked and mashed pumpkin, or canned
2/3 cup water
3-1/3 cups flour
2 tsp. baking soda
1 tsp. baking powder
1/2 tsp. salt
1 tsp. cinnamon
1 tsp. cloves
2/3 cup chopped walnuts
2/3 cup raisins

Preheat oven to 350°F. Cream butter and sugar. Add eggs, beat well, add pumpkin. Mix together all dry ingredients. Fold into pumpkin mix alternating with water. Add nuts and raisins. This large recipe makes 2 spring form tube pans or two 9 x 4 inch loaf pans plus 6 muffins. Bake about 50 minutes, slightly longer for loaf pans, less of muffins.

Note: *Keeps well in refrigerator and stays moist longer.*

SHRIMP SPREAD

PREPARATION TIME: 15 MINUTES
REFRIGERATION TIME: 24 HOURS
YIELD: 1 QUART

1-1/2 lb. shrimp, cooked and peeled
1 small onion, chopped
1 pkg. (8 oz.) cream cheese, softened
1/4 cup mayonnaise
Juice of 1 lemon
1 tsp. Worcestershire
1/8 tsp. Tabasco or hot sauce
Pinch cayenne pepper
Salt to taste
6 Tblsp. butter or margarine, melted
Garnish: Parsley flakes

Reserve 4 whole shrimp. Place remaining ingredients except parsley into food processor and mix until smooth. Refrigerate 24 hours before serving. Garnish with parsley and reserved shrimp. *Serve with crackers or fresh vegetable slices.*

CRAWFISH BITES

PREPARATION TIME: 5 MINUTES
COOKING TIME: 5 MINUTES
SERVES: 4 - 6

1 lb. crawfish tails, cooked and cut into 1 inch pieces
1/4 lb. butter
2 cloves garlic, minced, or 1/4 tsp. garlic powder
Salt and pepper to taste

Sauté meat in butter and seasonings, turning occasionally until lightly browned. *Serve with a mixture of ketchup and horseradish.*

HOT CRAB MEAT

PREPARATION TIME: 5 MINUTES
COOKING TIME: 20-30 MINUTES
SERVES: 4 - 6

1 can (6-1/2 oz.) crab meat, drained
1 pkg. (8 oz.) cream cheese, softened
1 Tblsp. milk
2 Tblsp. minced onion or 1 Tblsp. dehydrated chopped onion
1 tsp. horseradish
1 tsp. Tabasco or hot sauce
1 Tblsp. Worcestershire sauce
Salt and pepper to taste
Paprika

Preheat oven to 350°F. In a large bowl, combine ingredients, except paprika. Place in baking dish and sprinkle with paprika. Bake 20 to 30 minutes. *Serve hot with crackers.*

FRESH COCONUT CHIPS

PREPARATION TIME: 10 MINUTES
COOKING TIME: 5 MINUTES
SERVES: 4

Coconut
Melted butter
Salt to taste

Crack coconut and remove meat. Slice coconut meat into thin chips and toss lightly with melted butter. Place on baking sheet and broil until golden brown. Sprinkle lightly with salt and *serve warm.*

HOT SEAFOOD SPREAD

PREPARATION TIME: 5 MINUTES
COOKING TIME: 15-20 MINUTES
YIELD: 1-3/4 CUPS

1 pkg. (8 oz.) cream cheese, softened
1 can (6-1/2 oz.) or fresh cooked crab meat, drained*
2 Tblsp. dry sherry
1 tsp. lemon juice
Dash hot pepper sauce
1/2 cup sliced almonds

Preheat oven to 350°F. In a medium bowl, combine cream cheese, crab meat, sherry, lemon juice, and pepper sauce. Place in a shallow baking dish. Sprinkle almonds evenly over mixture. Bake 15 to 20 minutes until hot and bubbly. *Serve with crackers.*

*Also try using cooked and shredded lobster, crawfish, or surimi crab meat.

BREADFRUIT CHIPS

PREPARATION TIME: 5 MINUTES
COOKING TIME: 10 MINUTES
SERVES: 4

1 full firm breadfruit, peeled and cut into quarters
Water
Vegetable oil for frying

Place breadfruit in a saucepan. Add boiling water to cover. Cook until tender. Drain. Cut into very thin slices. Fry in hot oil. Drain on paper towel.

CURRY DIP

PREPARATION TIME: 5 MINUTES
REFRIGERATION TIME: OVERNIGHT
YIELD: 1 CUP

1 cup mayonnaise
1 tsp. curry powder or more to taste
1 tsp. dry mustard
1 tsp. garlic salt
1 tsp. wine vinegar
1 tsp. prepared mustard
1 tsp. fresh onion, grated
Garnish: 2 tsp. fresh chopped parsley (optional)

Blend all ingredients in food processor or by hand. Refrigerate overnight. *Serve with crackers and fresh vegetable slices.*

Hint: *For a tasty alternative, add 2 cups cooked shredded crawfish.*

SPICY AVOCADO DIP

PREPARATION TIME: 15 MINUTES
COOKING TIME: NONE
YIELD: 2 - 3 CUPS

3 ripe avocados, peeled and quartered
1/2 medium onion, minced
1 tomato, peeled an quartered
1 Tblsp. fresh lemon juice
1 Tblsp. Tabasco or hot sauce
1 tsp. Worcestershire sauce or to taste

Place all ingredients in food processor. Blend until smooth. *Serve with potato or tortilla chips.*

Note: *Place an avocado seed in blended dip to prevent discoloring.*

CREAMY AVOCADO DIP

PREPARATION TIME: 10 MINUTES
COOKING TIME: NONE
SERVES: 4 - 6

4 large avocados, peeled and seeded
4 Tblsp. sour cream
2 oz. cream cheese
1 clove garlic
Salt to taste
Dash of Worcestershire sauce

Place first four ingredients in food processor and mix until smooth. Add salt and Worcestershire sauce to taste. *Serve as a dip with crackers or as a spread for finger sandwiches.*

TRADITIONAL CONCH FRITTERS

PREPARATION TIME: 10 MINUTES
COOKING TIME: 20 MINUTES
SERVES: 4 - 6

1 egg, beaten
1 cup flour
3/4 tsp. baking powder
Salt and pepper
1 tsp. Tabasco or hot sauce
2 large conch, including the orange mantle, cleaned and finely diced
1/2 green bell pepper, finely chopped*
1 onion, finely chopped
1 celery stalk
1/4 cup milk or water
Vegetable oil for frying

Mix the egg, flour, baking powder and seasonings with enough milk or water to make a stiff batter. Mix in remaining ingredients and allow to stand for 15 minutes before deep frying. Drop by teaspoonful into hot oil and fry until golden brown. *Serve with Bahamian Red Sauce (page 66) or Tartar Sauce (page 65) and a cold beer.*

* For a variation use red bell pepper.

CONCH CEVICHE

PREPARATION TIME: 5 MINUTES
MARINATING TIME: 30 MINUTES
SERVES: 4

2 conch, pounded and sliced very thinly across the grain
1/2 medium onion, thinly sliced
1/4 cup fresh lime juice
1/4 cup water
Dash of Tabasco or hot sauce
Salt and pepper to taste

Combine water, lime juice, Tabasco, salt and pepper. Place conch and onion slices in a shallow glass dish. Pour liquid over conch. Allow to marinate at least 30 minutes in the refrigerator or at room temperature. Drain and *serve with toothpicks.*

CRAWFISH PASTE

PREPARATION TIME: 10 MINUTES
CHILLING TIME: 4 HOURS
SERVES: 20+

2 lbs. cooked crawfish meat, shredded
1/4 lb. butter
3 Tblsp. mayonnaise
1 tsp. lemon juice
1/4 tsp. celery salt
1 tsp. Worcestershire sauce
3 drops of Tabasco or hot sauce, to taste
1/4 tsp. pepper

Combine crawfish, butter and mayonnaise until well blended. Season with remaining ingredients. Place in a bowl and chill 4 hours or overnight. *Serve with crackers.*

Mama's Mango Salsa

Preparation time: 20 minutes
Chilling time: Overnight
Serves: 4

4 fresh mangos, peeled, seeded and diced
1 jalapeño pepper, seeded and chopped, or to taste
1 small red pepper, diced
2 green onions, finely diced
1/4 cup olive oil
1/4 cup chopped fresh cilantro leaves
2 cloves garlic, minced
2 Tblsp. lime juice
Salt and pepper to taste

In a large bowl, combine all ingredients and mix well. Refrigerate overnight. Try this delicious salsa over grilled foods. It also makes a wonderful dip served with corn chips.

CASSAVA BALLS

PREPARATION TIME: 20 MINUTES
COOKING TIME: 25-30 MINUTES
SERVES: 6 - 8

3 medium cassavas (about 1 lb. each)
1/2 tsp. pepper
1 tsp. salt

Peel the cassavas and cut into small pieces. Place in a pot and cover with water. Add pepper and salt. Cover, bring to a boil and simmer 25 to 30 minutes or until cassava is soft. Drain. Place cassava in a food processor and blend until the mixture comes away from the side of the bowl and forms as ball. Moisten palms of you hands and roll mashed cassava into little balls. Arrange on a platter and cover until ready to serve.

BLACK BEAN DIP

PREPARATION TIME: 10 MINUTES
COOKING TIME: NONE
SERVES: 6

1 can (15 oz.) black beans, drained
1 Tblsp. chili powder
1/2 tsp. cumin
1 Tblsp. fresh lemon juice
1/4 cup chopped onion

In a food processor, purée beans. Add remaining ingredients and blend. *Serve with sliced garden vegetables or tortilla chips.*

Variation: *To make Red Bean Dip, substitute red kidney beans for black beans.*

FIRE DANCE FRITTERS

PREPARATION TIME: 10 MINUTES
COOKING TIME: 20 MINUTES
SERVES: 6

1-1/2 cups crawfish meat, or lobster, cooked and ground
1-1/3 cups flour
2 tsp. baking powder
1/4 tsp. salt
1/4 tsp. paprika
1/4 tsp. cayenne pepper
1 egg, beaten
2/3 cup milk
Oil for frying

Sift together dry ingredients. In a separate bowl, combine lobster, egg, and milk. Add crawfish mixture to dry ingredients and mix. Drop by tablespoon into deep hot oil and fry until brown.

Pumpkin Fritters

PREPARATION TIME: 15 MINUTES
COOKING TIME: 30 MINUTES
SERVES: 6 - 10

2 cups flour
1 tsp. baking powder
Pinch of salt
3/4 cup brown sugar
3 eggs
1/2 cup milk
1 tsp. vanilla
2 cups cooked, mashed pumpkin
1/2 cup cooked raisins (optional)
Vegetable oil for frying

Sift flour, baking powder and salt together. Cream sugar and eggs; add milk and vanilla. Stir in pumpkin. Fold in raisins dredged in flour. Heat oil and drop batter by teaspoon. Fry 2-3 minutes per side until brown, turning once. *Serve alone or with sour cream dip.*

PINEAPPLE MAMA

PREPARATION TIME: 1 MINUTE
SERVES: 1

1-1/2 oz. white rum
2 oz. pineapple juice
1 oz. condensed milk
1/2 oz. Grenadine syrup
1 cup crushed ice
Garnish: 1 slice of fresh pineapple and 1 maraschino cherry

Blend all ingredients with crushed ice until creamy. *Serve in a highball glass and garnish with pineapple and cherry.*

PIÑA COLADA

PREPARATION TIME: 1 MINUTE
SERVES: 1

2 oz. pineapple juice
1 oz. coconut cream (Coco Lopez)
2 oz. light rum
1 cup crushed ice
Garnish: 1 slice of fresh pineapple and 1 maraschino cherry

In a blender, blend all ingredients until creamy. *Pour into a tall glass and garnish with pineapple and cherry.*

Junkanoo Rum Drink

PREPARATION TIME: 1 MINUTE
SERVES: 1

2 oz. light rum
2 oz. grapefruit juice, or lime, lemon, orange
3 tsp. simple syrup (see below)
1/4 of slice lime
Pinch of fresh ground nutmeg

In a short glass, combine rum, juice and simple syrup. Fill glass with ice. Add lime and a pinch of nutmeg. *Serve.*

Simple Syrup

PREPARATION TIME: 1 MINUTE
COOKING TIME: 5 MINUTES

2 cups sugar
1 cup water

In a saucepan, bring sugar and water to a boil. Boil 5 minutes. Cool; pour into a jar and refrigerate until needed.

BAHAMA MAMA DAIQUIRI

PREPARATION TIME: 5 MINUTES
SERVES: 4 - 6

4 oz. lemonade concentrate, or limeade
1 oz. Grenadine syrup
1 cup light rum
Ice

In a blender, place lemonade concentrate, grenadine syrup and rum. Add enough ice to make 5 cups. Blend until smooth. *Serve in a tall glass*

Note: *This recipe freezes well, so make it ahead of time!*

PAPAYA COCKTAIL

PREPARATION TIME: 5 MINUTES
SERVES: 4

1 medium papaya, peeled and diced
Juice of 4 oranges (about 1-1/3 cups)
2 tsp. sugar
Pinch of salt
1/4 cup maraschino cherry juice
Garnish: 4 maraschino cherries

Stir ingredients together. Pour into chilled cocktail glasses. *Serve with one cherry on top of each.*

BAY STREET PUNCH

PREPARATION TIME: 5 MINUTES
SERVES: 8 - 10

1 cup lime juice
1 cup simple syrup (see page 29)
1-1/2 cups rum, may substitute vodka or whiskey
Dash of Angostura bitters
2 cups crushed ice
Garnish:
1 banana, peeled and sliced
1 orange, sliced
Mint sprigs

In a blender, at medium speed, combine the lime juice, syrup, rum, bitters, and ice until smooth. *Serve in attractive glasses and garnish.*

RUM PUNCH

PREPARATION TIME: 5 MINUTES
SERVES: 4 - 6

4 cups tea, brewed
4 cups dark rum
1 cup sugar
12 lemons, sliced
Ice

While tea is still warm, add sugar and stir until dissolved. Pour into a punch bowl. Add rum, lemons. and ice. *Serve in individual glasses with ice.*

BEACH PARTY RUM PUNCH

PREPARATION TIME: 20 MINUTES
SERVES: 100+

1 (30-gallon) trash can, new or *very* clean
10 gallons water
3 gallons tea, very strongly brewed
3 gallons dark rum
18 cups lemon juice or 9 (16 oz.) bottles
10 lbs. sugar
30 lbs. ice
48 lemons, limes and/or sour oranges, sliced

Into trash can, pour water, warm tea and rum. Blend together. In a large bowl, combine sugar and lemon juice. Add to mixture. Add citrus slices and stir well. Add enough ice to chill. Add more ice as necessary.

Yellow Bird

PREPARATION TIME: 2 MINUTES
SERVES: 1

1-1/2 oz. rum
3 oz. pineapple juice
1/4 oz. orange juice
3/4 oz. creme de banana
Dash of Galliano
1/4 oz. apricot brandy

Shake well and *serve in a tall glass.*

Goombay Smash

PREPARATION TIME: 2 MINUTES
SERVES: 1

1-1/2 oz. dark rum
3/4 oz. coconut rum
3 oz. pineapple juice
1/4 oz. lemon juice
1/4 oz. triple sec
Dash of simple sugar (see page 29)
Garnish: Maraschino cherry and a lemon wedge

Shake well and *serve in a tall glass with cracked ice, a cherry and a wedge of lemon for garnish.*

GINGER 'N SPICE COOLER

PREPARATION TIME: 2 MINUTES
SERVES: 1

4 oz. Chardonnay wine (may use alcohol-free)
2 oz. ginger ale
2 dashes Angostura Bitters
Garnish: Lemon peel

Stir and serve over ice in a wine glass. Garnish.

RUM SOUR

PREPARATION TIME: 2 MINUTES
SERVES: 1

2 oz. rum
1 tsp. sugar
Juice of 1/2 lemon or lime
Garnish: 1/2 slice of lemon and a maraschino cherry

Shake with ice and strain into a glass. Garnish.

OLE NASSAU

PREPARATION TIME: 2 MINUTES
SERVES 1

3/4 oz. coconut rum
1-1/4 oz. gold rum
3 oz. pineapple juice
2 oz. evaporated milk
Dash of simple syrup (see page 29)

Shake well and serve in a tall glass with ice.

CARIBBE

PREPARATION TIME: 1 MINUTE
SERVES: 1

1 oz. white rum
1 oz. gin
1/2 oz. lime juice
1 tsp. sugar
Garnish: 1 slice orange

Shake together with ice. Strain over rocks in a prechilled old-fashioned glass. Garnish with an orange slice.

Rum Splash

Preparation time: 2 minutes
Serves 1

1-1/2 oz. rum
1/2 oz. Amaretto
1/2 oz. sour mix
1/2 oz. orange juice
1/2 oz. cranberry juice
1/2 oz. grapefruit juice
1/2 oz. pineapple juice
1/2 oz. Grenadine
Garnish: Maraschino cherry, orange or fresh pineapple

Shake sour mix and juices together. Pour mixture into a hurricane glass and continue to layer ingredients in order, finishing with Grenadine. Serve with a straw and garnish with a cherry speared to a wedge of orange or fresh pineapple.

Rum-Dinger

Preparation time: 1 minute
Serves: 1

1-1/2 oz. white rum
2 oz. cream
1 oz. pineapple juice
1/4 oz. Grenadine
1/2 fresh banana
Garnish: Pineapple slice

Place all ingredients in a blender. Mix until smooth. Pour into a fluted glass and garnish with a pineapple slice.

Soursop

Preparation time: 1 minute
Serves: 1

1-1/2 oz. white rum
1 oz. soursop nectar
1 Tblsp. fresh lime juice
Ice

Shake all the ingredients well. Strain into prechilled cocktail glasses. *Serve icy cold.*

Soursop-Banana Daiquiri

Preparation time: 2 minutes
Serves: 1

1-1/2 oz. white rum
1/4 oz. dark rum
1 oz. soursop nectar
1/4 oz. lime juice
1/2 cup sliced banana
1/3 cup crushed ice
Garnish: Maraschino cherry

Place all ingredients in blender. Blend 10 to 15 seconds. Pour into a prechilled daiquiri glass. Garnish.

Bahama Mama

PREPARATION TIME: 2 MINUTES
SERVES: 1

3/4 oz. dark rum
1/2 oz. Nassau Royale or 1/4 oz. Grand Marnier
1/4 oz. Cointreau
2 oz. orange juice
Dash Angostura Bitters
1/2 oz. Grenadine
1/4 oz. lemon juice
Garnish: Orange slice and a maraschino cherry

Shake with cracked ice. *Serve in a tall glass.* Garnish with an orange slice and a cherry.

Conch Shell

PREPARATION TIME: 1 MINUTE
SERVES: 1

4 oz. white rum
1/2 oz. lime juice

Shake well with ice. Strain over rocks in a prechilled old-fashioned double glass.

MAMA'S HOMEMADE "KAHLUA"

PREPARATION TIME: 5 MINUTES
COOKING TIME: 10 MINUTES
AGING TIME: 30 DAYS
YEILD: 8 - 10 CUPS

4 cups boiling water
4 cups sugar
1 cup instant coffee granules
4 cups vodka
2 Tblsp. pure vanilla extract
1 (1 inch) vanilla bean section

In a pot, simmer water, sugar and coffee for 10 minutes. Remove from heat. Stir in vodka, vanilla extract and bean. Pour in a dark bottle and age 30 days.

PERFECT PAPAYA

PREPARATION TIME: 3 MINUTES
SERVES: 3 - 4

1 cup fresh papaya chunks, chilled
1 Tblsp. fresh lime juice
1 cup mango nectar, chilled
2 tsp. sugar or sugar substitute
1 cup crushed ice
Ice water
9 - 12 ice cubes

Place papaya chunks, lime juice, mango nectar and sugar in blender. Blend until smooth. Stop blender and add crushed ice. Blend until smooth. Add ice water to bring liquid up to 20 ounces. Place 3-4 ice cubes in each glass. Divide liquid evenly between glasses and *serve immediately.*

BEE'S KISS

PREPARATION TIME: 1 MINUTE
SERVES: 1

1-1/2 oz. white rum
1 Tblsp. black coffee
1 Tblsp. fresh cream

Shake and blend with ice.

Coconut, Carrot and Raisin Salad

Preparation time: 10 minutes
Cooking time: 5 minutes
Serves: 4

1 cup coarsely grated coconut
3 medium carrots, coarsely grated
1/2 green bell pepper, chopped
1/4 cup raisins
1/2 tsp. fine herbs
1/2 cup orange juice
3 Tblsp. mayonnaise
3 Tblsp. milk
1/4 tsp. paprika
Salt and pepper to taste

Mix coconut, carrots and pepper together. In a saucepan, bring raisins to a boil in the orange juice. Cool. Mix the mayonnaise and milk. Add to vegetables and combine thoroughly. Season to taste. *Serve chilled.*

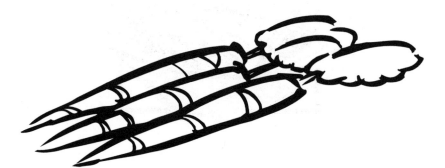

CRAWFISH SALAD

PREPARATION TIME: 10 MINUTES
CHILLING TIME: 30 MINUTES
SERVES: 2 - 4

1 cup cooked, flaked crawfish meat or lobster
1 small onion, finely chopped
2 tsp. lemon juice
2 Tblsp. mayonnaise
Salt and pepper to taste
1 tsp. hot pepper sauce or to taste
1/2 tsp. paprika
1 head lettuce
1 cucumber, sliced
4 small sweet pickles, sliced
1 avocado, sliced

In a bowl, combine crawfish meat, onion, lemon juice, mayonnaise, salt, pepper, hot pepper sauce, and paprika. Chill. Arrange serving plates with a bed of lettuce, cucumber, sweet pickles and avocado. Place a portion of the crawfish mixture in the center. Chill before serving.

Junkanoo Salad

PREPARATION TIME: 15 MINUTES
CHILLING TIME: 30 MINUTES
SERVES: 6-8

3/4 cup mayonnaise
1 small onion, finely chopped or grated
1/4 tsp. white pepper
2 breadfruits, peeled, boiled and cut into bite size pieces
2 cans (15 oz.) green peas, drained or frozen peas
2 cans (15 oz.) diced cooked carrots, drained or frozen
4 tomatoes, sliced
6-8 lettuce leaves

In a small bowl, mix together mayonnaise, onion and pepper. (If using frozen vegetables, add a pinch of salt). In a large bowl, combine vegetables and dressing. Chill. Arrange a lettuce leaf and sliced tomato on each serving plate. Place a serving of the salad in the center.

Breadfruit Salad

PREPARATION TIME: 10 MINUTES
CHILLING TIME: 30 MINUTES
SERVES: 4-6

3 breadfruits, peeled, boiled and cut into bite size pieces
1/2 cup diced celery
1 hard boiled egg, mashed
1 tsp. prepared mustard
1 cup mayonnaise
1 tsp. sugar
1 Tblsp. vinegar
Salt and pepper to taste

Combine all ingredients together. Chill before serving.

CONCH SALAD
(LAMBI)

PREPARATION TIME: 30 MINUTES
CHILLING TIME: 2-3 HOURS
SERVES: 6

4 fresh conch, cleaned and tenderized
2 onions, chopped
1 green bell pepper, seeded and chopped
Juice of 4 or 5 fresh limes or sour oranges
1/4 tsp. salt
1/2 tsp. black pepper
Hot sauce to taste
1 Tblsp. chopped pimento
2 tomatoes, diced

Dice conch. Place in bowl with onion, green pepper, lime juice, salt and pepper. Marinate in the refrigerator for 2-3 hours. Just before serving, add tomatoes, pimentos and hot sauce.

ANOTHER CONCH SALAD

PREPARATION TIME: 15 MINUTES
CHILLING TIME: 2 HOURS
SERVES: 6 - 8

4-5 conch, cleaned, tenderized, and cut in small pieces
1 medium onion, chopped
1/2 cup chopped green bell pepper
2 Tblsp. chopped pimento
1 tsp. chopped parsley
1 clove garlic, minced
1/2 cup sour orange juice or lime juice
1 Tblsp. vinegar
1 tsp. Worcestershire sauce
1/4 cup olive oil
Dash of Tabasco
1/2 tsp. salt
1/2 tsp. oregano
1/2 tsp. thyme
Garnish: Lettuce leaves

In a large bowl, combine conch, onion and pepper. In a small bowl combine remaining ingredients. Pour over mixture in large bowl. Chill at least 2 hours. *Serve on lettuce leaves.*

Note: *This salad also makes a great hors d'oeuvre; serve with crackers.*

TROPICAL FRUIT SALAD

PREPARATION TIME: 30 MINUTES
CHILLING TIME: 1 HOUR
SERVES: 6 - 8

2 large ripe papayas, peeled and sliced
2 ripe avocados, peeled and sliced
6 ripe tomatoes, peeled and sliced
1 small red onion, sliced into thin rings
1 head lettuce (red tip or Romaine)

DRESSING:
1 clove garlic, crushed
1 coddled egg (boil for 1 minute), lightly beaten
Juice of 1/2 lemon
1/2 cup light cream
1/4 tsp. sugar
1/2 tsp. dry mustard
1 tsp. tarragon
5 Tblsp. vinegar
1/2 cup + 2 Tblsp. vegetable oil
1 tsp. salt
1/2 tsp. white pepper
1/2 tsp. black pepper

In a bowl, whisk together the ingredients for dressing. Place in a jar with a tight fitting lid. Let sit 1 hour to allow flavors to blend. Artistically arrange fruits and vegetables in sections on a lettuce lined platter. Chill. When ready to serve, shake dressing vigorously and pour over sliced fruits and vegetables.

Note: *This salad platter is absolutely beautiful.*

COLD CURRIED SALAD

PREPARATION TIME: 20 MINUTES
CHILLING TIME: OVERNIGHT
SERVES: 4 - 6

1 lb. crawfish, cooked and flaked
1 apple, cored and chopped
1/2 green bell pepper, seeded and chopped
4 green onions, chopped
1 ripe avocado, peeled, seeded and cubed
1/2 cup peanuts or cashews
Salt and pepper to taste
2/3 cup mayonnaise
1/3 cup sour cream
1 Tblsp. curry powder
4 cups cooked rice, chilled

In a large bowl combine crawfish, apple, green pepper, green onions, avocado, peanuts, salt and pepper. Mix together mayonnaise, sour cream and curry powder. Gently toss one half of the dressing with crawfish mixture. Place a portion of cold rice on each plate and top with salad. *Serve remaining dressing on the side.*

Note: *This is also delicious using cooked, cubed chicken instead of the crawfish.*

CREAMY CUCUMBER AND ONION SALAD

PREPARATION TIME: 10 MINUTES
CHILLING TIME: 30 MINUTES
SERVES: 4 - 6

3 small cucumbers, thinly sliced
2 medium onions, thinly sliced
1/2 cup mayonnaise
1/4 cup coarsely chopped parsley
1-1/2 tsp. lemon juice
1/2 tsp. sugar
Salt and pepper to taste

In a large bowl, combine all ingredients. Chill before serving.

Hint: *For a more eye appealing presentation, cut slivers in the cucumbers' skin or score with a fork.*

Avocado and Pineapple Salad

Preparation time: 15 minutes
Chillng time: 30 minutes
Serves: 3 - 4

2 large ripe avocados
6-8 slices pineapple, fresh is preferred
Garnish: Lettuce leaves

Dressing:
1/3 cup ripe avocado, mashed
2/3 cup mayonnaise or sour cream
1-1/2 Tblsp. fresh lime juice
Dash of Tabasco
Salt and pepper to taste

In a bowl, combine mashed avocado, mayonnaise, lime juice, Tabasco, salt, and pepper. Stir together until creamy. Chill at least 30 minutes. When ready to serve, place a bed of lettuce leaves on a platter. Cut, peel and slice the avocado. Arrange the sliced avocado and pineapple on top of the lettuce and pour the chilled dressing over the salad.

Note: *For a creamier dressing add more mayonnaise and lime juice. Sour cream in place of mayonnaise creates a bolder dressing.*

Calypso Salad

PREPARATION TIME: 15 MINUTES
CHILLING TIME: 30 MINUTES
SERVES: 4

2 cups shredded white cabbage
2 Tblsp. diced ham or bacon
1/2 cup chopped cooked chicken breast
1/2 cup shredded carrots
1/2 cup finely chopped onions
1 sweet red pepper, diced
3/4 cup mayonnaise
4 oz. cheddar cheese, shredded or sliced
1/2 cup sultanas or raisins
1/2 cup chopped pecans

In a large bowl, mix cabbage, ham, chicken, carrots, onions, and red pepper together with mayonnaise. Chill. Before serving sprinkle with cheese, sultanas and pecans.

CRAB 'N SHRIMP SALAD

PREPARATION TIME: 15 MINUTES
CHILLING TIME: 1 HOUR
SERVES: 4 - 6

1 large head iceberg lettuce, shredded
1/2 cup finely chopped green onions
1 cup chopped celery
1/2 lb. crab meat, cooked and flaked
3/4 lb. small shrimp, cooked and cleaned
Garnish: 2 medium tomatoes, cut in wedges

DRESSING:
2/3 cup mayonnaise
5 cloves garlic, finely minced
2 Tblsp. + 1 tsp. lemon juice
1 tsp. white pepper
Dash of Tabasco
1/2 tsp. salt
2 tsp. fresh dill
2 Tblsp. minced white onion

In a jar with a tight lid, combine dressing ingredients and chill at least 1 hour.

Toss lettuce, onion and celery with 1/4 cup of dressing. Add crab and shrimp. Toss. Divide among chilled salad plates. Garnish with tomato wedges. *Serve with the remaining dressing on the side.*

OKRA SOUP

PREPARATION TIME: 10 MINUTES
COOKING TIME: 2 HOURS
SERVES: 6

1 medium ham bone, with ample meat remaining
10 cups water
2 lbs. fresh okra, sliced thin
1 clove garlic, chopped
1 large onion, coarsley chopped
1 green bell pepper, chopped
3 Tblsp. tomato paste
1 can (16 oz.) tomatoes, chopped
1/2 cup long grain rice, uncooked
1/4 tsp. thyme
1/4 tsp. salt
Pepper to taste

In a large pot, cover ham bone with water. Add 1/4 tsp. salt and simmer over low heat 1-1/2 hours. Add the remaining ingredients. Cook an additional 30 minutes. *Correct seasoning and serve.*

LAND CRAB SOUP

PREPARATION TIME: 10 MINUTES
COOKING TIME: 2 HOURS 35 MINUTES
SERVES: 6

6 large white land crabs, washed
2 Tblsp. olive oil
1 large onion, chopped
3 Tblsp. tomato paste
1 Tblsp. flour
1 tsp. thyme
1/4 cup rice, uncooked
2 potatoes, cut in chunks
2 large carrots, cut in chunks
8 cups water, boiling

Cook crabs (uncracked) in 2 tablespoons water over low heat about 30 minutes or until crabs turn red and water is evaporated. Turn crabs occasionally, so as not to burn. Remove from heat. Crack the shells, pick out the meat and fat and discard shells. In a large pot, heat oil and sauté onion, tomato paste, flour and thyme. Stir constantly until onions are cooked. Add crab meat and claws. Stir 1 minute. Add boiling water and remaining vegetables. Simmer 2 hours. *Serve hot.*

COLD CUCUMBER SOUP

PREPARATION TIME: 10 MINUTES
CHILLING TIME: 1 HOUR
SERVES: 6

2 cans (10-3/4 oz.) condensed cream of celery soup, undiluted
1 large cucumber, peeled, seeded and chopped
2 Tblsp. watercress, chopped
1 green onion, chopped
2 cups milk
Dash of Tabasco or hot sauce
1 cup sour cream
Garnish: Paprika and scored cucumber slices

In a food processor, purée soup, cucumber, watercress and onion. Remove from processor to a bowl and stir in milk and Tabasco. Chill one hour. Pour into bowls and top each with a spoonful of sour cream. *Sprinkle with paprika and place scored cucumber slices on top.*

CRAWFISH BISQUE

PREPARATION TIME: 10 MINUTES
COOKING TIME: 20 MINUTES
SERVES: 4

1-1/2 cups crawfish meat, cooked and flaked
4 cups milk
1/2 small onion, sliced
2 stalks celery, sliced
1 sprig parsley
1 bay leaf
1/3 cup melted butter
1/3 cup flour
1/2 tsp. salt
1/2 tsp. white pepper
1/4 cup sherry
Garnish: Croutons

Scald milk with onion, celery, parsley, and bay leaf. Strain. In a large saucepan, combine butter with flour, salt and pepper over low heat until a paste forms. Using a whip, slowly stir in scalded milk. Continue cooking, stirring constantly, until thickened. Add crawfish and sherry; heat through. *Serve hot with croutons.*

Goombay Conch Chowder

Preparation time: 30 minutes
Cooking time: 2 hours
Marinating time: 1 hour
Serves: 6 - 8

1 lb. conch, tenderized, chopped or processor ground
4 Tblsp. lime juice
6 strips bacon, chopped
2 medium onions, chopped
2 cloves garlic, chopped
3 stalks celery (with tops), chopped
3 cans (14-1/2 oz.) chicken broth
1 bottle clam juice
2 bay leaves
1 tsp. Worcesershire sauce
2 dashes Tabasco or hot sauce
1/3 cup sherry
2 cups new potatoes, peeled and cubed
1 can (16 oz.) chopped tomatoes
1/4 tsp. paprika
2 tsp. chopped parsley
1/2 tsp each of oregano, basil, thyme, and turmeric

Marinate chopped conch in lime juice for 1 hour. Strain juice, reserving 2 tablespoons. Set conch and reserved juice aside. In a large kettle, cook bacon until almost crisp. Add onion, garlic and celery and sauté until tender. Add broth, clam juice, bay leaves, Worcestershire sauce, Tabasco, sherry, and potatoes. Stir to blend and simmer briefly. Add tomatoes, conch and seasonings. Simmer 1-1/2 hours. Remember to adjust the seasoning to your taste. *Serve with a dash of hot pepper sauce on top of each serving.*

CRAWFISH GUMBO

PREPARATION TIME: 15 MINUTES
COOKING TIME: 35-40 MINUTES
SERVES: 6

2 Tblsp. butter
1 large onion, chopped
2 cloves garlic, chopped
1/2 cup celery, chopped
1/4 cup parsley, chopped
1/2 cup carrots, chopped
3 medium tomatoes, chopped
1/4 cup flour
6 cups chicken broth
10 oz. frozen okra, sliced
Salt and pepper, to taste
1 lb. crawfish meat, diced

In a pot, melt butter over low heat and add onion, garlic, celery, carrot and tomatoes. Sauté gently until vegetables are tender, stirring occasionally. Sprinkle flour over the mixture and blend well. Gradually stir in chicken broth, okra and parsley. Increase heat and bring to a boil, stirring occasionally. Lower heat and simmer 5 minutes. Add crawfish and simmer 5-10 minutes longer. *Season and serve hot.*

GREEN TURTLE SOUP

PREPARATION TIME: 15 MINUTES
COOKING TIME: 2 HOURS
SERVES: 6 - 8

2 lbs. turtle meat, chopped
8 cups water
2 Tblsp. vegetable oil
1 medium onion, chopped
2/3 cup celery, cut fine
1/2 cup fresh okra, diced
1 medium bell pepper, chopped
2 cups tomatoes, chopped
2 Tblsp. tomato paste
4 large potatoes, diced
2 carrots, diced
2 Tblsp. Worcestershire sauce
1/4 tsp. thyme
Salt and pepper to taste
4 oz. pasta noodles, uncooked
1/2 cup sherry

Place turtle meat into a large pot. Add boiling water to cover and cook 20 minutes. Drain. In a skillet, heat oil and add onion, celery, okra, and bell pepper. Sauté until light brown, stirring to prevent burning. Add tomatoes and tomato paste. Mix well. Add this mixture to the turtle. Add 8 cups fresh boiling water. Stir well. Add remaining ingredients, except noodles. Simmer 1-1/2 hours, or until turtle is tender. During the last 20 minutes, add noodles. *Correct seasoning and serve. Add sherry just before serving.*

Note: *The green turtle is an endangered species. However, in the Bahamas it is still served, in season, as a delicacy. This recipe was not tested in the preparation for this book. We have included this recipe for Green Turtle Soup because of its authenticity only and do not recommend the harvesting of any endangered species.*

White Conch Chowder

Preparation time: 15 minutes
Marinating time: 30 minutes
Cooking time: 1 hour 10 minutes
Serves: 4

2 large conch, including the orange mantle
1/3 cup fresh lime juice
1/2 tsp. salt
2 slices bacon, chopped
2 medium onions, chopped
2 cloves garlic, minced
1 potato, chopped
3 stalks celery, sliced
3 carrots, sliced
3 cups water
3 chicken bouillon cubes
2 Tblsp. lime juice
Salt and pepper to taste
1 Tblsp. chopped parsley
2 Tblsp. white wine
1 can (6 oz.) evaporated milk

Grind conch in a food processor. Stir in lime juice and 1/2 tsp. salt. Set aside to marinate 30 minutes. Sauté bacon and add onions, garlic, potato, celery, and carrots. Add the conch and stir fry for a few minutes. Add water and bouillon. Simmer 1 hour. Season to taste. Add parsley, wine and milk before serving.

SWEET POTATO AND CARROT SOUP

PREPARATION TIME: 10 MINUTES
COOKING TIME: 30 MINUTES
SERVES: 4

2 medium onions, finely chopped
4 Tblsp. butter
1 lb. carrots, thinly sliced
1 lb. sweet potatoes, thinly sliced
2 cups vegetable stock
1-1/2 cups milk
Thyme to taste
Salt and pepper to taste

In a skillet, sauté onions in butter until soft. Add carrots and sweet potatoes. Cook, stirring constantly until all butter is absorbed. Add the stock. Cover and simmer until the vegetables are tender, about 20 minutes. Strain. Stir in milk and add thyme, salt and pepper. Heat through. Do not boil.

"Pepper Pot"
(Beef, Crawfish and Vegetable Soup)

Preparation time: 15 minutes
Cooking time: 1 hour 10 minutes
Serves: 6 - 8

1 lb. stewing beef, cubed
1/2 lb. salt pork, chopped
8 cups water
1 lb. spinach, chopped
1 lb. greens (mustard, collard, turnip), chopped
1 large onion, chopped
3 cloves garlic, chopped
1 hot pepper, chopped
1/2 lb. sweet potatoes, chunked
1/2 lb. cassava, chunked
Salt and pepper, to taste
12 small okra, cut in rings
2 Tblsp. butter
2 Tblsp. coconut cream
1/4 lb. crawfish meat, chopped

In a large pot, place beef and pork in 6 cups water. Cover and simmer 1 hour. In a separate pot, boil spinach and greens with 2 cups water until tender. Place the greens and water in a food processor and purée. Add puréed greens to beef and salt pork pot. Add onion, garlic, hot pepper, sweet potato and cassava. Season with salt and pepper. Simmer until vegetables are tender and soup thickens. Sauté okra in butter 10-15 minutes until tender. Add okra, crawfish and coconut cream and cook 5 minutes longer.

Avocado Soup

PREPARATION TIME: 10 MINUTES
CHILLING TIME: 30 MINUTES
SERVES: 4

2 large ripe avocados, peeled, pitted and cubed
4 cups lemon yogurt
2 cups milk, or 1 cup milk plus 1 cup light cream
1/2 cup scallions, minced
1 Tblsp. dry sherry
1/2 tsp. salt
Garnish: Fresh mint leaves

Place all ingredients in food processor. Blend until smooth. Chill. Garnish with mint leaves.

Tomato Shrimp Soup

PREPARATION TIME: 5 MINUTES
COOKING TIME: 10 MINUTES
SERVES: 6 - 8

8 cups chicken broth
4 medium tomatoes, coarsely chopped
2 cups English cucumber, peeled, seeded and cut into 1/4" strips
2 cups shrimp meat, cooked

In a stock pot, bring chicken broth just to boiling. Add tomatoes and simmer 2 minutes. Add cucumber and shrimp and simmer until heated through.

Note: *This is a low fat, low calorie soup. Use homemade chicken broth instead of canned for lower sodium and fat content.*

PAPAYA PEPPER SAUCE

PREPARATION TIME: 15 MINUTES
COOKING TIME: 10 MINUTES
YIELD: 4 CUPS

1 small green papaya, boiled, peeled and chopped
1/2 lb. hot peppers, seeded and crushed
1 medium cucumber, chopped
2 medium onions, finely chopped
2 garlic cloves, minced
1 Tblsp. salt
2 cups vinegar
1 Tblsp. prepared mustard
1 tsp. olive oil

In a large saucepan, combine all ingredients and simmer over medium heat for 10 minutes. Allow to cool before serving. Use as a condiment or dipping sauce. *Stores well in jars.*

TARTAR SAUCE

PREPARATION TIME: 5 MINUTES
COOKING TIME: NONE
YEILD: 1 CUP

2/3 cup mayonnaise
2 tsp. Dijon mustard
2 tsp. minced onion
2 tsp. finely chopped parsley
1 tsp. capers, chopped
1 tsp. pickle relish
3 stuffed olives, chopped
1 hard boiled egg, finely chopped

Mix all ingredients together. For a thinner sauce, add a little lemon juice.

"Old Sour" Sauce

PREPARATION TIME: 5 MINUTES
MARINATING TIME: 7-10 DAYS

1 cup fresh lime, sour orange or lemon juice
1 Tblsp. salt
1 hot pepper
1 chili pepper or cayenne to taste

Place ingredients in a clean bottle with tight lid. Shake well and leave at room temperature for 7-10 days. This sauce will keep indefinitely unrefrigerated. Use on conch and in dressings.

Note: *Traditionally this sauce has been used as a substitute for fresh citrus in conch recipes. "Old Sour" is prepared and stored during the citrus season for use until the following season.*

Bahamian Red Sauce

PREPARATION TIME: 5 MINUTES
COOKING TIME: NONE
YEILD: 2/3 CUP

1/2 cup ketchup
1/4 tsp. salt
1/4 tsp. pepper
2 Tblsp. Worcestershire
2 Tblsp. lime juice
Dash of Tabasco or to taste

Mix all ingredients together.

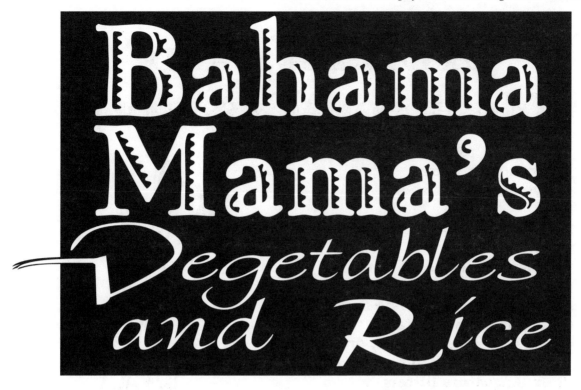

Asparagus and Mushroom Casserole

Preparation time: 15 minutes
Cooking time: 1 hour
Serves: 4

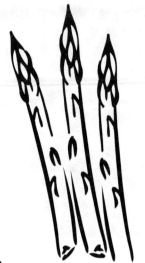

1 large package egg noodles
4 oz. butter
2 Tblsp. whole wheat flour
2-1/2 cups milk
Salt and pepper to taste
Cayenne pepper to taste
1 can (15 oz.) asparagus, drained
1 lb. fresh mushrooms, sliced
2 oz. Angostura Bitters
1 cup grated Romano cheese or Parmesan
1 tomato, sliced
Garnish: Parsley

Preheat oven to 350°F. In a large pot, cook noodles according to directions on package, about 7 minutes. Drain and set aside in colander. In the same pot, melt butter and stir in the flour. Cook 1 minute. Add milk and season with salt, pepper and cayenne. Add asparagus, mushrooms and noodles. Mix well, adding the Angostura Bitters. Pour into a casserole dish. Top with cheese and tomato slices. Bake 40 minutes. Garnish with parsley.

Note: *You may also use canned mushrooms, sweet corn, artichoke hearts or any available vegetable. The "magic ingredient" is the Angostura Bitters.*

PEAS AND RICE

PREPARATION TIME: 5 MINUTES
COOKING TIME: 30 MINUTES
SERVES: 6 - 8

2 slices of bacon, cut small
1 medium onion, chopped
1-1/2 cups rice, uncooked
1 can (15 oz.) blackeye peas (retain liquid)
1 small tomato, chopped
1-1/2 tsp. tomato paste
1 cup water
1 tsp. dried thyme
Salt and pepper, to taste

In a large pan with a tight fitting lid, fry bacon. Add onions and cook until clear, about 5 minutes. Stir in rice and cook 1 minute. Add peas with liquid, tomato, tomato paste, water, thyme, salt, and pepper. Stir gently to mix. Bring to a boil. Lower heat and cover. Cook until rice is tender, about 20 minutes.

Modern Mama's Alternative: *Replace bacon with 1 Tblsp. olive oil.*

PIGEON PEAS

PREPARATION TIME: 10 MINUTES
COOKING TIME: 1 HOUR 15 MINUTES
SERVES: 4 - 6

2 cups dried pigeon peas
1 tsp. salt
2 slices of bacon, chopped
1 small sweet red bell pepper, chopped
1/2 cup onion, finely chopped
1/2 tsp. dried oregano
1/2 tsp. dried thyme
2 Tblsp. butter
1/2 tsp. black pepper

In a saucepan, cover peas with water, add 1/2 tsp. salt. Stir, cover and boil peas until cooked, about 1 hour. Drain, rinse and set aside. Fry bacon in pan. Add peppers, onion, remaining 1/2 tsp. salt and herbs. Cook until onions are clear. Return peas to pan and heat through. Remove from heat, stir in butter and season with pepper.

CORN PUDDING

PREPARATION TIME: 15 MINUTES
COOKING TIME: 1 HOUR
SERVES: 4 - 6

2 cans (16 oz.) cream style corn
2 cups evaporated milk
4 eggs, beaten
6 slices of bread, chopped small
1/2 cup whole milk
1 Tblsp. sugar
1/4 lb. butter
1 stalk celery, chopped
1 small onion, chopped
1 green bell pepper, chopped
1 cup shredded cheddar cheese
1/2 tsp. paprika

Preheat oven to 350°F. Melt butter in saucepan. Add onion, celery and bell pepper. Sauté until lightly browned. Add remaining ingredients except cheese and paprika. Mix well. Place into a 2 quart casserole dish and sprinkle with cheese and paprika. Bake 1 hour.

Stuffed Tomatoes

Preparation time: 15 minutes
Cooking time: 30 minutes
Serves: 6

1 Tblsp. vegetable oil
1 medium onion, finely chopped
2 cloves garlic, crushed
1 celery stalk, finely chopped
1 small green bell pepper, finely chopped
1 tsp. dried oregano
1/2 tsp. salt
1 tsp. lemon juice
1 lb. ground beef
1/3 cup bread crumbs
6 medium tomatoes

Preheat oven to 350°F. In a skillet, heat oil. Add onions, garlic, celery, green pepper, oregano, salt, lemon juice and meat. Sauté until meat is crumbled. Drain. Stir in bread crumbs. Cut tops off tomatoes. Scoop out and finely chop the inside of tomatoes. Add chopped tomatoes to the mixture. Adjust seasoning to taste. Fill tomato shells with the meat mixture. Place in a well greased casserole dish and bake 15 minutes. *Serve hot.*

Hint: *Try sprinkling shredded cheese on tomatoes after baking. Return to oven until cheese melts.*

CURRIED PUMPKIN

PREPARATION TIME: 10 MINUTES
COOKING TIME: 30 MINUTES
SERVES: 4

1/4 cup vegetable oil
2 medium onions, thinly sliced
1 Tblsp. curry powder or to taste
2 lbs. pumpkin, peeled, cut in 1/2" thick slices
2 cups water
1/2 tsp. salt
1 tsp. white pepper
1 Tblsp. lemon juice

In a pot, heat oil. Sauté onion until clear. Stir in curry and pumpkin and sauté a few more minutes. Add water, salt, pepper and lemon juice. Simmer until cooked, about 15-20 minutes.

FRIED PLANTAINS

PREPARATION TIME: 10 MINUTES
COOKING TIME: 8-10 MINUTES
SERVES: 4

2 lbs. ripe plantains, peeled and cut in halves lengthwise
1 egg, beaten
1/2 cup milk
1/2 cup flour
1/2 lime
Oil for frying

In a skillet, heat oil. Squeeze lime juice over plantain halves. Mix a batter of egg, milk and flour. Dip each plantain half in batter. Fry until brown on both sides. Drain on paper towels.

CARIBBE EGGPLANT

PREPARATION TIME: 15 MINUTES
COOKING TIME: 45 MINUTES
SERVES: 6 - 8

2 eggplants, peeled and thinly sliced
1/4 cup shredded coconut
Milk of 1 fresh coconut
1/2 cup milk
1/8 tsp. salt
1/4 tsp. pepper
1/8 tsp. fresh nutmeg, grated
1/2 onion, cut into rings

Preheat oven to 300°F. Soak eggplant slices in hot salted water for 10 minutes, drain and set aside. In a saucepan, combine shredded coconut, coconut milk, milk, salt, pepper, and nutmeg. Bring to a boil and cook 10 minutes. Layer onion rings and eggplant in a greased casserole. Strain milk mixture and discard shredded coconut. Pour seasoned milk over eggplant and onion. Bake 30 minutes.

MARINATED CARROTS

PREPARATION TIME: 10 MINUTES
COOKING TIME: 10-12 MINUTES
COOLING TIME: 30 MINUTES
SERVES: 8

3 lbs. carrots, sliced
1 green bell pepper, finely chopped
2 cloves garlic, minced
1 can (6 oz.) condensed tomato soup, undiluted
1/4 cup vegetable oil
1 medium onion, thinly sliced in rings
1 tsp. dry mustard
1 Tblsp. Worcestershire sauce
1/3 cup sugar
1/2 cup cider vinegar
Salt and pepper to taste

In a large pot, place carrot slices and cover 3/4 with water. Cook until crisp tender. Drain and set aside. Heat remaining ingredients, except onion, until just boiling. Add onion to carrots. Pour sauce over both, mixing well. Allow to cool 30 minutes. *Serve.*

Note: *Place in a covered plastic container for storage up to one month.*

Breadfruit Au Gratin

Preparation time: 15 minutes
Cooking time: 30-40 minutes
Serves: 6 - 8

4 Tblsp. + 2 Tblsp. butter
2 cups milk
6 Tblsp. flour
1 cup cheddar cheese, grated
1 breadfruit, cooked and diced
2 large onions, chopped
2 stalks of celery, chopped
Salt and pepper to taste

Preheat oven to 375°F. In a saucepan, melt 4 tablespoons butter over low heat. Add milk and flour. Stir until thick. Stir in cheese. Add breadfruit, onions, celery, salt and pepper. Mix. Pour mixture into a greased casserole dish. Dot with remaining butter. Bake 20-30 minutes.

Boiled Breadfruit

Preparation time: 5 minutes
Cooking time: 15-20 minutes
Serves: 6 - 8

1 firm breadfruit
Water

Peel breadfruit and cut into cubes or slices. Place in a saucepan and cover with boiling water. Cook until tender when pierced with a fork, about 15 minutes.

Option: *You may also roast a breadfruit. Preheat oven to 350°F. Slice breadfruit in half. Place skin side up in a shallow baking dish and bake for 30-40 minutes or until tender. Peel skin prior to eating.*

Onion Casserole

PREPARATION TIME: 15 MINUTES
COOKING TIME: 45-50 MINUTES
SERVES: 6 - 8

6 large onions, sliced thin
1 cup milk
4 Tblsp. butter, melted
2 Tblsp. flour
1/4 lb. cheddar cheese, grated
1/4 lb. fresh mushrooms, sliced
Salt and white pepper to taste
1/2 cup bread crumbs

Preheat oven to 350°F. Cook onions in boiling water until tender. Drain. In a saucepan, combine milk, 2 Tblsp. butter and flour. Heat, stirring constantly, until thickened. Add cheese and mushrooms to the white sauce; mix well. Season to taste. In a greased casserole dish, layer onions and sauce. Repeat. Top with bread crumbs and drizzle with remaining butter. Bake 30 minutes.

"Old Timey" Peas and Rice

Preparation time: 5 minutes
Cooking time: 20-30 minutes
Serves: 8 - 10

1/2 lb. bacon, chopped
1 large onion, chopped
2 stalks of celery, chopped
1/2 medium green bell pepper, chopped
2 cans (16 oz.) pigeon peas, drained
3 cups rice, uncooked
1 can (6 oz.) tomato paste
1 can (16 oz.) whole tomatoes
3 cups water
1/2 tsp. dried thyme or to taste
Salt and pepper to taste

Fry bacon until crisp. Add onion, celery and bell pepper and sauté until softened. Add remaining ingredients. Stir. Bring to a boil and allow to boil 5 minutes. Reduce heat to lowest setting. Cover and continue cooking 20-30 minutes or until rice is cooked.

Modern Mama's Alternative: *Substitute 1/4 cup olive oil for bacon.*

GRAND LUNCHEON

PREPARATION TIME: 10 MINUTES
COOKING TIME: 20 MINUTES
SERVES: 4

2 Tblsp. vegetable oil
1 large onion, sliced
1 red bell pepper, cored, seeded and sliced
1 green pepper, cored, seeded and sliced
2 cloves garlic, crushed
4 tomatoes, skinned and chopped
Salt and pepper to taste
4 large eggs, beaten
2 Tblsp. milk
4 slices french bread, toasted

Heat vegetable oil in a pan. Add onion and pepper. Sauté until softened. Add garlic, tomatoes, salt and pepper. Simmer 5 minutes. Beat eggs and milk together. Pour into pan and cook for 3-4 minutes, stirring occasionally. *Serve immediately over toast.*

Note: *Serve with a garden salad and a bowl of soup .*

Rice and Beans

Preparation time: 15 minutes
Cooking time: 30 minutes
Serves: 6 - 8

2 fresh coconuts, shredded
7-8 cups water
3/4 cup dried red kidney beans, washed
1/2 tsp. each of basil, oregano and thyme
2 cups rice, washed
Salt and black pepper

In a saucepan, add coconut to 4 cups water and bring to a boil. Remove from heat. Allow to steep 10 minutes. Drain and discard coconut flesh, reserving coconut water (milk). Return "milk" to saucepan and add beans. Bring to a boil and continue cooking until beans are tender. Add herbs, thyme, salt and pepper to taste. Stir in rice. Add enough water to cook rice (about 3-4 cups). Cover. Bring to a boil. Reduce heat and allow to simmer until rice is cooked. *Serve hot.*

CARROT AND LEMON BAKE

PREPARATION TIME: 10 MINUTES
COOKING TIME: 30-45 MINUTES
SERVES: 4

1/2 lb. butter
1/2 cup brown sugar
1 lemon
1 egg, beaten
1-1/4 cups grated carrots
1-1/4 cups flour
Salt to taste
1 tsp. baking powder
1/2 tsp. baking soda
Garnish: Slices of lemon and sprigs of mint

Preheat oven to 350°F. In a bowl, combine butter and sugar until creamy. Juice lemon and grate zest. Add to bowl and mix in remaining ingredients. Place in greased baking dish and bake 30-45 minutes. Remove from oven and garnish. *Serve hot.*

BAHAMA RICE

PREPARATION TIME: 10 MINUTES
COOKING TIME: 25-30 MINUTES
SERVES: 4 - 6

1 medium white onion, diced
2 Tblsp. butter or oil
1 large carrot, diced
2 green onions, finely chopped
1/4 tsp. turmeric
1/2 tsp. curry powder
2 cloves
1/8 tsp. salt
1/4 tsp. pepper
1/4 tsp. cayenne pepper
2 cups rice, washed and drained
4 cups water
1 cup frozen peas

Sauté onion in butter until clear. Add remaining ingredients (except water and peas). Sauté gently for a few minutes, stirring to prevent rice from burning. Add water, cover and cook 15-20 minutes. Stir in peas. Cook until rice is tender and liquid is absorbed.

Island Conch Stew

Preparation time: 20 minutes
Cooking time: 40 minutes (Pressure Cooker)
Serves: 4

4 medium conch, cleaned, pounded and cut in pieces
1/4 lb. salt pork or bacon, chopped
3 large onions, 1 chopped and 2 quartered
Water
2 large carrots, cut in chunks
3 large potatoes, cut in chunks
3 stalks celery, cut in chunks
Sprig fresh thyme or 1 tsp. dried
Sprig fresh parsley or 1 tsp dried
1 bay leaf
2 large garlic cloves, minced
2 Tblsp. flour
2 Tblsp. catsup
1 Tblsp. Worchestershire sauce
1 Tblsp. malt vinegar
1/4 cup dark rum
Squeeze of lime juice
Salt and pepper to taste

Sauté pork in pressure cooker with 1 chopped onion. When golden, add conch and water to cover. Cook thirty minutes. Add remaining onions, carrots, potatoes, thyme, parsley, bay leaf, and garlic. Cover with water and pressure cook an additional 5 minutes. Remove thyme and parsley sprigs and bay leaf. In a small bowl, combine the remaining ingredients. Add to stew and stir until thickened. *Serve hot with steamed rice.*

Famous Boiled Fish

Preparation time: 5 minutes
Cooking time: 15-20 minutes
Serves: 4 - 6

2-3 lbs. grouper or other fish
Water
Salt and pepper to taste
2 Tblsp. butter
2 Tblsp. hot sauce
Juice of 2 lemons, limes or sour orange
1 tsp. dried oregano
1 tsp. thyme
2 cloves garlic, chopped
2 onions, sliced
Additions: Potatoes, sweet potatoes, cassava

Clean and wash fish. Place in a heavy bottom saucepan and cover 3/4 with water. Add salt, pepper, butter, hot sauce, and lemon juice. Sprinkle with oregano, thyme and garlic. Place onions on top of fish and cook over medium heat until fish is tender. *Serve with crusty bread.* Potatoes, sweet potatoes or cassava, may be cooked with the fish.

Note: *Grouper is a favorite fish for "boiling" and the Bahamians are masters at cooking it to perfection. It should be tender and flaky with a mild flavor. Avoid cooking too long or the fish will fall apart.*

Baked Snapper

Preparation time: 5 minutes
Cooking time: 1 hour 20 minutes
Serves: 6

1 (3-4 lbs.) snapper fillet
1/2 lb. butter, melted
1/4 tsp. thyme
Salt and pepper to taste
1 large onion, chopped
2 Tblsp. tomato paste
3 cups bread crumbs

Preheat oven to 350°F. Place snapper fillet in a greased shallow baking dish. Baste with 1/4 lb. melted butter. Season with thyme, salt and pepper. Bake for 1 hour. Melt remaining butter in a skillet and add remaining ingredients. Cook for 15 minutes. Spread sauce over the fish. Return to oven and bake 20 minutes longer.

Beer Marinated Grouper

Preparation time: 5 minutes
Marinating time: 1 hour
Cooking time: 10 minutes
Serves: 6

3 lbs. grouper fillets, cut into 1" thick strips
24 oz. beer
1 cup flour
Salt and pepper
Vegetable oil, not more than 1/8" deep
Garnish: Tartar sauce and lemon slices

Marinate fish strips in beer for 1 hour. Dry fish well, pressing between paper towels. Heat 1/8" deep oil. Roll strips in seasoned flour and shake off excess flour. Fry quickly. about 10 minutes total, turning once. Drain on paper towels. *Serve with tartar sauce and lemon slices.*

GOLDEN GROUPER

PREPARATION TIME: 15 MINUTES
COOKING TIME: 10-15 MINUTES
SERVES: 8

8 portions of grouper fillets

SPICY MUSTARD SAUCE:
1/4 lb. butter
2 onions, chopped
2 cloves garlic, minced
Juice of 2 lemons, limes or sour oranges
3 Tblsp. spicy mustard
Salt and pepper to taste

Preheat oven to 350°F. Wash and pat dry grouper fillets; set aside. Melt butter in a saucepan. Add onions and sauté until clear; add garlic, lemon juice, mustard, salt and pepper. Place fillets in shallow baking dish. Spoon mixture over fillets and bake until fish is flaky, about 15 minutes.

Note: *Fillets may be cooked over the grill, turning them frequenty while brushing liberally with sauce. If your grill has a large grate, use screening material to keep fillets from falling into flame. Fish is done when inner most area is white and flaky. This sauce can used with any firm fish fillet.*

BAKED BONEFISH WITH TOMATOES

PREPARATION TIME: 10 MINUTES
COOKING TIME: 35 MINUTES
SERVES: 6

1 (5-6 lbs.) bonefish (do not remove scales)
Salt to taste
Juice of 2 limes
2 Tblsp. oil
2 onions, chopped
2 cloves garlic, chopped
1 tsp. oregano
2 fresh tomatoes, chopped
Garnish: Parsley sprigs and lemon slices

Preheat oven to 350°F. Season fish with salt and lime juice. Let stand 10 minutes or longer. Place fish in a greased shallow baking pan and bake 30 minutes or until tender. Sauté onions and garlic in oil until softened. Add oregano and tomatoes. Cook down to reduce liquid, stirring constantly. Pour sauce over fish. Return to oven for about 5 minutes. *To serve, lift fish from scales onto platter.* Garnish with parsley and lemon slices.

Savory Swordfish

PREPARATION TIME: 5 MINUTES
COOKING TIME: 20 MINUTES
SERVES: 6

6 swordfish steaks, cut 1" to 1-1/2" thick
Salt and pepper
Mayonnaise

Preheat broiler or grill. Season both sides of steaks. Spread mayonnaise generously on each side. Broil or grill about 5 minutes. Do not overcook. *Serve with tartar sauce (page 65) or lemon slices.*

Marinated Swordfish

PREPARATION TIME: 10 MINUTES
MARINATING TIME: 2 HOURS
COOKING TIME: 10 MINUTES
SERVES: 8

2 Tblsp. olive oil
1/4 cup soy sauce
1 Tblsp. dry white wine
1/4 cup fresh lemon juice or sour orange
3 garlic cloves, minced
1 small onion, chopped
1 tsp. marjoram or basil
1 tsp. ground black pepper
8 (6 oz.) pieces of swordfish, 3/4" thick

Mix together all ingredients, except swordfish, until well blended. Place swordfish in a shallow dish. Pour mixture over and marinate covered for 2 hours or longer, basting occasionally. Remove from marinade and cook under preheated broiler for approximately 5 minutes on each side.

Fish and Rice Casserole

Preparation time: 5 minutes
Cooking time: 35-40 minutes
Serves: 6

1-1/2 cups cooked and flaked fish, grouper, mahi mahi, etc.
3 Tblsp. onion, minced
4 Tblsp. butter
1-1/2 cups cooked rice
1 cup mild cheese, grated
2 eggs, lightly beaten
2 tsp. curry powder or to taste
1/4 tsp. Worcestershire sauce
Cayenne pepper to taste
Salt and pepper to taste
3 bananas, slightly under ripe, sliced
Garnish: Chutney

Preheat oven to 350°F. Sauté onions in 2 Tblsp. butter. Mix together all ingredients, except banana and chutney, adding them in order listed. Place mixture in greased baking dish and bake 35-40 minutes or until golden brown. Sauté banana in remaining 2 Tblsp. butter. *Serve with garnish of sautéed bananas and chutney.*

Fish and Corn Casserole

Preparation time: 10 minutes
Cooking time: 30 minutes
Serves: 6 - 8

1-1/2 lbs. grouper fillet or snapper, cooked and flaked
3 Tblsp. butter
3 Tblsp. flour
2 cups milk
1/4 tsp. dry mustard
Salt and pepper to taste
1 can (16 oz.) corn kernels, drained
2 eggs, separated
1/2 cup grated cheddar cheese
3 Tblsp. bread crumbs

Over low heat, melt butter in saucepan, stirring in flour to make paste. Add milk and bring to a boil, stirring constantly. Add mustard, salt and pepper. Simmer 2-3 minutes. Remove from heat and stir in corn. Beat in egg yolks and 1/4 cup cheese, reserving 1/4 cup cheese for the top.

Preheat oven to 350°F. Beat the egg whites until they hold a stiff peak. Fold into sauce. Grease baking pan or dish and fill with alternate layers fish and sauce, finishing with sauce. Mix the remaining cheese with the bread crumbs and sprinkle on top. Bake 20-25 minutes or until brown.

Hint: *You can prepare this dish earlier in the day and bake just before serving.*

BAKED MAHI MAHI WITH GARDEN VEGETABLES

PREPARATION TIME: 10 MINUTES
COOKING TIME: 25-30 MINUTES
SERVES: 4 - 6

2 lbs. mahi mahi fillet, in one piece
1/2 tsp. salt
1 tsp. pepper
1/4 cup fresh lemon juice
2 onions, peeled and sliced
2 tomatoes, peeled and sliced
1 green bell pepper, sliced
3-4 large mushrooms, sliced
2 sprigs fresh parsley, chopped
2 Tblsp. butter, melted

Preheat oven to 375°F. Sprinkle both sides of fish with salt and pepper. Place in a dish and sprinkle with lemon juice. Let stand for 10 minutes. Arrange half of the onions, tomatoes and green pepper in a greased baking dish. Add the fish and cover with remaining onion, tomato and bell pepper. Add mushrooms and parsley. Drizzle butter evenly over top. Bake 25 to 35 minutes, until fish can be flaked with a fork, basting several times.

Note: *Baking time varies with the thickness of the fish.*

FISH STEW

PREPARATION TIME: 15 MINUTES
COOKING TIME: 45 MINUTES
SERVES: 6 - 8

2 Tblsp. butter
1 medium onion, chopped
3 stalks celery, chopped
2 cloves garlic, minced
1/2 cup chopped parsley
1 can (32 oz.) tomatoes
2 cups V-8 juice or tomato juice
1/2 cup white wine
1 cup water
1 green bell pepper, chopped
3 bay leaves
1 tsp. basil
1 tsp. oregano
1/2 tsp. hot sauce
2 lbs. grouper fillets or other fish, cut into 1" chunks
Salt and pepper

Heat butter in a heavy bottom large saucepan. Sauté onion, celery and garlic until tender. Add all the other ingredients, except the fish, and simmer with lid on at least 30 minutes. Add fish and simmer 15 minutes more. *Serve with a huge salad and crusty bread.*

CRAWFISH MEDALLIONS IN GARLIC BUTTER

PREPARATION TIME: 15 MINUTES
COOKING TIME: 10 MINUTES
SERVES: 6 - 8

6 large crawfish tails, shelled
4 cloves fresh garlic, coarsely chopped
1/3 cup melted butter
Garnish: Fresh parsley, lemon or lime wedges dusted with paprika

Shell crawfish tails and retain meat. Trim and slice meat at diagonal to have slices to lay in the shape of the tail. Sauté garlic in butter until it begins to brown. Add crawfish slices. Cook a few minutes over high heat to keep crawfish from becoming tough. Do NOT overcook.

To serve, realign pieces of crawfish, overlapping to shape into tails. Drizzle with garlic butter, then garnish with fresh parsley and lemon wedges dusted with paprika.

BAHAMIAN LAND CRABS AND RICE

PREPARATION TIME: 10 MINUTES
COOKING TIME: 40 MINUTES
SERVES: 4 - 6

3 medium sized white land crabs, uncooked
3 Tblsp. bacon drippings, butter or oil
1 small onion, finely chopped
1 tsp. thyme
Dash hot sauce
Salt and pepper to taste
2 Tblsp. tomato paste
4 cups water
2 cups rice

Separate back from body of crab. Remove fat from body, discarding gall and back shell (take care not to break the bitter gall.) Set fat and body shell aside. Heat bacon drippings in a saucepan over medium heat. Add onion and sauté until light brown. Add thyme, hot sauce, salt, pepper, and tomato paste. Stir until well blended. Add water, rice, crabs and crab fat. Stir. Bring to a boil. Cover, reduce heat to low and cook 25 minutes. Do NOT uncover while rice is cooking.

Turtle Steaks

Preparation time: 15 minutes
Cooking time: 20 minutes
Serves: 4

4 (8 oz.) green turtle steaks
Juice of 1 lime
Worcestershire sauce
Salt and white ground pepper to taste
Flour
1/4 lb. butter
1 garlic clove, crushed
1 small onion, thinly sliced
1 small leek, white only, thinly sliced
2 green bell peppers, thinly sliced
1/4 cup pimento thinly sliced
1/4 cup sherry
Juice of 1 sour orange
Garnish: Chopped fresh parsley

Season steaks with salt, pepper, lime juice and Worcestershire sauce and dust with flour. Heat butter in skillet and fry steaks until brown. Remove steaks to a serving platter. Sauté garlic and vegetables. Add sherry and orange juice. Pour vegetables and sauce over steaks and sprinkle with parsley. *Serve with boiled potatoes and tomato slices.*

Note: *The green turtle is an endangered species. However, in the Bahamas it is still served, in season, as a delicacy. This recipe was not tested in the preparation for this book. We have included this recipe for Green Turtle Steaks because of its authenticity only and do not recommend the harvesting of any endangered species.*

FREEPORT FISH STUFFING

PREPARATION TIME: 10 MINUTES
COOKING TIME: 5 MINUTES
SERVES: 6 - 8

2 cups soft bread crumbs
1/3 cup melted butter
1 medium onion, minced
1 stalk celery, chopped fine
Pinch of salt
1/2 tsp. pepper
1 tsp. dry sage
Dash of hot pepper sauce
1 egg, well beaten
Optional: Chopped apple, raisins, dried apricot or mango, and nuts

In a bowl, pour 1/4 cup butter over bread crumbs and set aside. In a saucepan, sauté onion in remaining butter, browning lightly. Add onion mixture and remaining ingredients to bread crumbs. Mix well. Fill fish and bake as directed.

Note: *This may also be used to stuff meats or poultry.*

PORK TENDERLOIN

PREPARATION TIME: 5 MINUTES
COOKING TIME: 1 HOUR
SERVES: 6 - 8

2 pork tenderloins
1/2 cup Worcestershire sauce
1/2 cup Soy Sauce
1 cup honey
1 cup ketchup

Preheat oven to 350°F. Place tenderloins in a large baking pan and cook 30 minutes. Mix liquids together. Baste tenderloins. Continue baking an additional 30 minutes. *Serve remaining sauce over meat.*

BAKED CHICKEN

PREPARATION TIME: 10 MINUTES
COOKING TIME: 2-1/2 HOURS
SERVES: 4 - 6

1 chicken, cut up
3/4 cup orange juice
1 can cream of mushroom soup
1/2 cup water
1/2 cup white wine
1 cup long grain rice, uncooked
1 package dry onion soup mix

Preheat oven to 325°F. Combine orange juice, mushroom soup, water and wine in a bowl. Generously grease a 13 x 9 x 2 inch casserole dish and evenly sprinkle in the rice. Dip chicken into mixture in bowl. Lay chicken on rice. Pour remaining mixture over the chicken. Sprinkle top with dry soup mix. Cover pan lightly with foil. Bake 2-1/2 hours.

CURRIED CHICKEN AND TROPICAL FRUIT

PREPARATION TIME: 10 MINUTES
COOKING TIME: 40 MINUTES
SERVES: 4 - 6

2 chicken breasts, boneless and skinless, cut into 1/2" pieces
3 Tblsp. vegetable oil
1 medium onion, chopped
2 tsp. curry powder
Salt and pepper to taste
1/2 cup heavy cream
1 firm ripe papaya, cut into 1/2" cubes
1 mango, cut in 1/2" cubes
1/2 lb. seedless grapes, cut in halves
Garnish: Lettuce leaves, 1/4 cup of each fruit above

Heat oil in a large skillet. Sauté onion until clear. Add curry powder, salt and pepper. Increase heat, add chicken and cook until tender. Reduce heat. Stir in cream and cook until slightly thickened, stirring constantly. Set aside 1/4 cup of each fruit for garnish. Add remaining fruit to the skillet and cook until fruit is heated. Place lettuce leaves on serving platter. Place chicken and fruit mixture in middle and garnish with reserved raw fruit.

Hint: *Use roasted nuts and coconut flakes as an additional garnish.*

WEST END PIGEON

PREPARATION TIME: 20 MINUTES
COOKING TIME: 1-1/2 HOURS
SERVES: 6 - 8

8 white crowned pigeons, feathered and cleaned
Black pepper
3-1/4 lb. onions, diced
4 cups chicken broth
1 cup dry sherry
1/4 cup fresh parsley, diced
Vegetable oil for frying

Remove wings and legs. Split pigeons in half along back and breastbone. Sprinkle liberally with black pepper. Lightly brown pigeons in vegetable oil (about 20 minutes). Remove pigeons. Sauté onions in same pan until golden. Place pigeons back into skillet and cover with chicken broth and sherry. Add water until meat is 3/4 covered. Cover pan and simmer 45 minutes. Add water as it cooks away to prevent drying. Sprinkle in parsley and simmer another 15-20 minutes. *Serve with garbanzo beans.*

Mama's Best Chicken

PREPARATION TIME: 10 MINUTES
COOKING TIME: 45-60 MINUTES
SERVES: 4 - 6

1 large chicken, jointed
1 onion, sliced
1 stalk celery, chopped
3 potatoes, peeled and quartered
1/2 cup lime juice
2-3 cups water
2 bay leaves
Hot sauce to taste
Salt and pepper to taste

Place all ingredients in pot with water. Cover and cook over medium heat for 45-60 minutes or until meat is tender. *(Variation below)*

Mama's Best Pig Feet

PREPARATION TIME: 10 MINUTES
COOKING TIME: 45-60 MINUTES
SERVES: 4 - 6

3 lbs. pig feet, cleaned
1 onion, sliced
1 stalk celery, chopped
1/2 cup lime juice
2-3 cups water
3 potatoes, peeled and quartered
2 bay leaves
Hot sauce to taste
Salt and pepper to taste

Place all ingredients in pot with water. Cover and cook over medium heat for 45-60 minutes until meat is tender.

CHICKEN AND DUMPLINGS

PREPARATION TIME: 10 MINUTES
COOKING TIME: 1-1/2 HOURS
SERVES: 4 - 6

1 stewing chicken or 2 small fryers, about 6 lbs., jointed small
4 celery stalks with leaves, cut into 2" pieces
1 carrot, sliced
2 garlic cloves, chopped
1 medium onion, chopped
2-3 sprigs parsley
1 tsp. salt
1/2 tsp. pepper
1 bay leaf

DUMPLINGS:
1-1/4 cups flour, sifted
2 tsp. baking powder
1/2 tsp. salt
2 Tblsp. vegetable oil
1/2 cup milk
2 Tblsp. chopped parsley

Place chicken in a large pot or Dutch oven and add water to cover. Add the remaining ingredients. Cover and bring to a boil. Reduce heat and simmer 2-1/2 hours or until meat is tender. When chicken is nearly cooked, sift together 1 cup flour, baking powder and salt. Combine oil and milk; add with parsley to dry ingredients and stir to moisten. Drop from tablespoon onto chicken in simmering stock. Cover tightly and simmer 12-15 minutes. Do not lift cover while cooking. Remove dumplings and chicken to a hot serving dish. Keep hot. Add enough water to stock to make 5 cups of liquid. Stir 1/4 cup flour with 1 cup of the liquid. Whip until smooth. Gradually add to broth, stirring constantly to avoid lumps. Cook until thickened and *serve over chicken and dumplings.*

Spiced Chicken

Preparation time: **5** minutes
Cooking time: **1** hour
Serves: **4 - 6**

3-4 lbs. chicken pieces, skinless
1/4 cup vegetable oil
6 cloves garlic, sliced
1/2 cup tamari or soy sauce
1/4 cup honey
2 tsp. dry mustard or cayenne pepper
Tabasco to taste
Garnish: Sesame seeds

In a skillet, sauté chicken and brown in oil. Add garlic. In a bowl, mix the remaining ingredients to taste. Pour over chicken and cover. Cook over medium heat 30 minutes, basting occasionally. Uncover and cook 15 minutes more. Garnish with sesame seeds.

Whiskey Chicken

Preparation time: **5** minutes
Marinating time: Up to **2** hours
Cooking time: **40** minutes
Serves: **4 - 6**

3 lbs. broiler chicken, cut into pieces
1 lemon or lime, cut in half
1/4 cup whiskey
1/2 cup melted butter
2 Tblsp. soy sauce
1 Tblsp. ginger root
1 Tblsp. honey

Rub chicken pieces with the lemon. Mix other ingredients together. Marinate chicken up to 2 hours. Grill chicken 20 minutes on each side.

Mama's Spice Rub Chicken

Preparation time: 5 minutes
Cooking time: 35-40 minutes
Serves: 4

4 chicken breasts
1 tsp. ground cinnamon
1 tsp. anise seed, crushed
1/4 tsp. allspice, ground
1/8 tsp. cloves, ground
1/4 tsp. cayenne pepper or to taste
1/4 tsp. fresh ground black pepper
1/2 tsp. salt
2 Tblsp. vegetable oil
1 clove garlic, minced
3/4 cup pineapple juice, unsweetened

Combine spices. Rub over chicken breasts. In a skillet, heat oil and garlic. Add chicken and brown on both sides. Reduce heat. Add pineapple juice. Cover and simmer until done, about 35 minutes. *Serve.*

Hint: *Try grilling the chicken breasts for added flavor.*

Curried Pork and Pineapple

Preparation time: 10 minutes
Cooking time: 1 hour 15 minutes
Serves: 4

1 lb. pork, cubed and trimmed of fat
4 Tblsp. butter
1 medium onion, chopped
1 Tblsp. curry powder
1 cup water
1/2 tsp. salt
1-1/2 Tblsp. lemon juice
1 cup fresh pineapple chunks
1 cup fine white bread crumbs
4 cups cooked rice

In a skillet, melt 1 Tblsp. butter and sauté onion lightly. Add curry powder and continue to sauté until well blended. Add the pork and cook until brown, adding more butter if necessary. Carefully add the water and salt. Lower heat and cover. Simmer about 1 hour or until meat is tender. Add lemon juice.

While the meat is cooking, roll pineapple chunks in bread crumbs. Heat the remaining butter in a separate pan and lightly sauté the pineapple until golden. Pile the rice onto a serving platter. Pour the pork over the rice and place the fried pineapple on top.

Orange Ginger Ribs

Preparation time: 10 minutes
Cooking time: 25 minutes
Serves: 4

2 lbs. pork spareribs, separated into ribs, cut into 2" lengths
1/2 cup soy sauce
5 slices fresh ginger, about 1" circles
4 green onions, cut into 1/2" pieces
2 pieces of star anise, optional
1 cup chicken broth
1/2 cup sugar
4 tsp. chopped orange peel
1 Tblsp. minced fresh ginger
1 clove garlic, minced
2 Tblsp. vegetable oil

In a large pot, combine ribs, 1/4 cup soy sauce, sliced ginger, green onions, star anise and water to cover. Cover pot and simmer until ribs are cooked through, about 20 minutes. Remove from heat and cool to room temperature. Drain ribs.* Heat oil in large skillet over high heat. In a bowl, whisk together chicken broth, sugar, orange peel, ginger, garlic and remaining 1/4 cup soy sauce. Place ribs and broth mixture into skillet. Stir-fry until liquid is reduced, about 5 minutes.

Note: *Ribs can be prepared 1 day ahead. Cover and refrigerate.*

Pork Shanks with Vegetables

Preparation time: 10 minutes
Cooking time: 1 hour 30 minutes
Serves: 4

4 pork shanks
1 Tblsp. vegetable oil
4 large carrots, cut diagonally in 1/2" pieces
4 stalks celery, cut diagonally in 1" pieces
4 small onions, peeled and cut in half
1/4 cup water
1/2 tsp. salt
Pepper to taste

In a heavy skillet, heat oil until very hot. Brown the shanks. Lower heat, cover with a close fitting lid, and braise about 30 minutes. Add the carrots, celery, onion, water and seasonings. Cover and cook 40-50 minutes or until tender. *Serve meat on a platter surrounded with the vegetables.*

Hint: *Thicken remaining liquid for gravy or serve as is.*

Mama's Beef Patties
(World Famous Pastries)

PREPARATIONS TIME: 15 MINUTES
COOKING TIME: 40-50 MINUTES
SERVES: 10 - 15

1-1/2 lbs. ground beef
2 Tblsp. vegetable oil
3 large onions, finely chopped
3 scallions, finely chopped
2 scotch bonnet peppers, minced
1/2 cup celery, finely chopped
1/4 cup red bell pepper, diced
2 garlic cloves, minced
1 tsp. thyme, ground
1 tsp. turmeric
1 tsp. paprika
1 tsp. parsley flakes
2 tsp. black pepper or to taste
Salt to taste
3/4 cup fine bread crumbs
1 Tblsp. flour
1/4 cup cold water
Frozen pastry dough, thawed, cut in 5" circles

Preheat oven to 400°F. In a large skillet, heat oil and sauté beef, onions, scallions, peppers, celery, bell pepper and garlic until meat is browned and crumbly. Drain. Add seasonings, bread crumbs, flour and water. Stir and heat about 5 minutes. Cool to room temperature. Spoon one tablespoon of filling onto each pastry circle. Moisten edges of pastry and seal the edges by crimping with a fork. *Bake 20-30 minutes on ungreased baking sheets. Serve hot.

*Hint: For shiny patties, brush with beaten egg yolk before baking.

 Mango Cheesecake

Preparation time: 20 minutes
Chilling time: 1 hour
Serves: 6 - 8

25-30 graham cracker biscuits, crushed
1/4 lb. butter, melted
1/4 lb + 3/4 lb. cream cheese, softened
1/2 oz. unflavored gelatin
1/2 cup boiling water
1/2 cup mango, puréed
1/2 cup sour cream
1/2 cup sugar
1 tsp. lemon juice
1 tsp. vanilla
2 eggs, separated
Garnish: Sliced mango or mandarin orange sections

Mix crackers and melted butter together. Press into base and sides of 9 inch pie pan. Cool. Spread 1/4 lb. cream cheese into crust. Sprinkle gelatin into hot water and leave to dissolve. In a separate bowl, beat together mango, 3/4 lb. cream cheese, sour cream, sugar, lemon juice, vanilla, and egg yolks. Mix in the dissolved gelatin. Beat egg whites until stiff. Fold into cream mixture. Pour into crust base and chill to set. Garnish before serving.

Note: *A prepared cooked pie crust or graham cracker crust may be used in place of the crust prepared here. For a low fat pie, use nonfat or reduced-fat cream cheese and sour cream.*

Hint: *Add a drop of red and yellow food coloring to the batter to enhance the orange tint of the pie.*

RENDEZVOUS CAKE

PREPARATION TIME: 20 MINUTES
COOKING TIME: 1 HOUR 10 MINUTES
SERVES: 8 - 10

1-1/2 cups all purpose flour
1-1/2 cups whole wheat flour
1 tsp. salt
1 tsp. baking soda
1 tsp. allspice, ground
2 cups granulated sugar
1 can (8 oz.) crushed pineapple in juice
1/4 cup fresh lime juice
Zest of 3 limes
1-1/2 cups vegetable oil
3 eggs, beaten
1 cup chopped pecans or walnuts
Garnish: Powdered sugar, mint sprigs, slices of lime

Preheat oven to 350°F. Butter the sides of a bundt pan and set aside. In a large bowl sift together the flour, salt, baking soda, allspice, and sugar. In a separate bowl, mix the pineapple, lime juice, lime zest, oil, and eggs. Stir into the flour mixture. Add pecans and mix well. Pour into pan and bake until inserted toothpick comes out clean (about 1 hour 10 minutes). Remove from oven. Cover loosely with foil and allow to cool in pan. Turn out onto cake plate. Cover with patterned lace and dust with powdered sugar. Remove lace and garnish with mint sprigs and slices of lime.

RUM SPICE COOKIES

PREPARATION TIME: 10 MINUTES
COOKING TIME: 10 MINUTES
YIELD: 4 DOZEN

1 Tblsp. dark rum
1/2 cup unsalted butter, softened
1 cup packed brown sugar
2 eggs
2 cups cake flour
1 tsp. baking powder
1/2 tsp. salt
1 tsp. cinnamon, ground
1/4 tsp. cloves, ground
1/4 tsp. freshly grated nutmeg
1 cup seedless raisins, chopped
1 cup dates, chopped
1/2 cup unsalted cashew nuts or macadamia nuts, chopped

Preheat oven to 350°F. Grease baking sheets and set aside. In large bowl, mix together rum, butter and brown sugar until creamy. Beat in the eggs one at a time. Sift together the flour, baking powder, salt, cinnamon, cloves and nutmeg. Add to the rum butter mixture. Blend in the raisins, dates and nuts. Drop by the teaspoon onto prepared baking sheets (allow for 4" cookies). Bake until brown, about 10 minutes. Do *not* over bake. Allow to cool on a wire rack.

Note: *For your own special recipe, try adding more rum, dried fruits, coconut, candied pineapple or candied mango.*

Hint: *These are wonderful as soon as they come out of the oven. You will find they are even better if allowed to "rest" for a few days in an airtight container.*

MAMA'S COOKIES

PREPARATION TIME: 10 MINUTES
COOKING TIME: 15 MINUTES
SERVES: 8 - 12

2 cups rolled oats
1/2 cup sugar
3/4 cup coconut
1/4 lb. butter, melted
1 tsp. baking powder

Preheat oven to 350°F. Mix all ingredients together. Press into a 9" x 6" lightly greased baking dish. Cook 15 minutes or until golden brown. Cool slightly and slice into squares. Remove and cool on a wire rack. *Store in an airtight container.*

BRANDY FREEZE

PREPARATION TIME: 10 MINUTES
CHILLING TIME: OVERNIGHT
SERVES: 8 - 16

1 cup macaroons, crumbled
1/2 cup good brandy, to taste
1 gallon premium vanilla ice cream, softened
Garnish: Toasted almond slices, sprigs of mint

Mix all ingredients together. Freeze overnight. Serve in sherbet glasses, garnishing each serving with toasted almond slices and a sprig of mint.

BANANA PUDDING
(Mama's Secret Recipe)

PREPARATION TIME: 5 MINUTES
COOKING TIME: 15 MINUTES
SERVES: 6

3 Tblsp. all purpose flour
Pinch of salt
3/4 + 1/4 cup sugar
1 egg + 3 eggs separated
2 cups milk
1 tsp. vanilla extract
Vanilla wafers
5-6 bananas, sliced
Garnish: Shredded coconut

Preheat oven to 425°F. In a double boiler, combine flour, salt and 3/4 cup sugar. Mix in 1 whole egg and 3 egg yolks. Stir in the milk. Cook uncovered over boiling water, stirring constantly until thickened. Remove from heat. Add vanilla.

Line 1-1/2 quart casserole with vanilla wafers, then layer sliced bananas, then layer the custard. Repeat ending with custard. Beat remaining 3 egg whites until stiff, but not dry. Gradually add remaining 1/4 cup sugar and beat until mixture forms stiff peaks. Pile on top of pudding, covering entire surface. Place casserole on a baking sheet and bake 5 minutes or until slightly brown (watch closely). *Serve warm or chilled.* Sprinkle with shredded coconut.

Note: *You may also prepare this pudding in custard cups.*

COCONUT BLENDER PIE

PREPARATION TIME: 10 MINUTES
COOKING TIME: 40 MINUTES
SERVES: 6 - 8

2 cups milk
1-3/4 cups sugar
1/2 cup Bisquick
4 eggs
1/4 cup butter
1-1/2 tsp. vanilla extract
1 package (7 oz.) flaked coconut

Preheat oven to 350°F. In a blender, combine milk, sugar, Bisquick, eggs, butter, and vanilla. Blend 2 minutes on low. Stir in coconut. Pour into a greased 9 inch pie pan. Let stand 5 minutes. Bake 40 minutes. Allow to cool. *Serve at room temperature or chilled.*

APPLE CASSEROLE

PREPARATION TIME: 10 MINUTES
CHILLING TIME: 1 HOUR
SERVES: 6

4-6 apples, cored and diced
1/2 cup light Karo syrup (or 1/2 cup sugar + 1/2 cup water)
1 cup brown sugar
1 cup flour
1/2 cup butter
Cinnamon, ground

Preheat oven to 350°F. Place apples in a buttered casserole dish and top with syrup. Mix brown sugar, flour and butter until crumbly. Place over apples. Sprinkle with lots of cinnamon and bake 1 hour.

EASY LIME PIE

PREPARATION TIME: 20 MINUTES
COOKING TIME: 10 MINUTES
SERVES: 6 - 8

4 eggs, separated
1 can sweetened condensed milk
1/2 cup fresh lime juice
1/2 tsp. cream of tartar
1/2 cup sugar
1 (9 inch) baked pie shell or graham cracker crust
Garnish: Lime slices or zest of lime

Preheat oven to 350°F. Beat egg whites with cream of tartar until stiff. Slowly add sugar while beating. Whip until whites hold stiff peaks. In a separate bowl, blend egg yolks and milk until well mixed. Slowly add lime juice, mixing well. Pour into baked crust. Top with meringue. Bake 10 minutes or until meringue is lightly browned. Cool. *Serve chilled.*

FRUIT COMPOTE

PREPARATION TIME: 15 MINUTES
CHILLING TIME: 1 HOUR
SERVES: 6 - 8

8 small sweet seedless oranges, peeled and sectioned
1 can (16 oz.) crushed pineapple
1 cup strawberries, sliced
1 mango, peeled and chopped
2 cups flaked coconut
1 cup orange juice
1 cup coconut cream

In a clear glass bowl, layer fruits. Combine orange juice and coconut cream. Pour over fruit. Chill 1 hour.

ISLAND DELIGHT

PREPARATION TIME: 15-20 MINUTES
CHILLING TIME: 2-3 HOURS
SERVES: 6 - 8

2 bananas
3/4 cup fresh orange juice
1 medium size fresh pineapple, peeled, cored and cubed
2 fresh papayas, peeled, seeded and cubed
1 fresh mango, peeled, pitted and chopped
Garnish: 1/2 cup grated coconut

In a food processor, purée the bananas and orange juice. In a large bowl, combine the pineapple, papaya and mango. Layer fruit and banana purée into tall dessert glasses. Cover and chill several hours to blend flavors. Before serving, sprinkle with coconut.

PAPAYA CREAM

PREPARATION TIME: 10 MINUTES
CHILLNG TIME: 30 MINUTES
SERVES: 4

1 large papaya (about 2 lbs.), peeled, seeded, and quartered
2 cups plain yogurt
2 Tblsp. honey
1 Tblsp. lime juice
Garnish: Small papaya slices

In a food processor, combine papaya, yogurt, honey and lime juice. Blend until smooth. Pour into stemmed glasses and chill. Garnish with papaya slices before serving.

Note: *This refreshing dessert is easy to make and low in calories if you use nonfat yogurt.*

GUAVA DUFF

PREPARATION TIME: 15 MINUTES
COOKING TIME: 3 HOURS
SERVES: 6 - 8

10 oz. Bisquick
1/4 tsp. salt
1 cup flour
1 Tblsp. sugar
1/4 lb. butter
3 oz. vegetable shortening
Ice water
2 cups guava pulp or homemade guava jam
1/2 tsp. nutmeg
1/2 tsp. cinnamon
Milk
Sugar

Preheat oven to 350°F. Mix together the Bisquick, salt, flour and sugar. Cut the butter and vegetable shortening into the mixture. Gradually add a little ice water until it becomes a pastry consistency. With a rolling pin, roll out the dough to 3/4 inch thickness so that the width is the length of a loaf pan.

Spread the dough with guava pulp and sprinkle with nutmeg and cinnamon to one inch inside the edges. Moisten edges and roll up width-wise, pinching sides together.

Place in a greased loaf pan, brush top with milk and sprinkle on a little sugar. Bake 45 minutes or until the sides and top are browned. Allow to cool and slice while it is slightly warm. *Serve with Butter-Egg or Hard Sauce (see pages 121 and 122).*

Esther's Guava Duff

PREPARATION TIME: 20 MINUTES
COOKING TIME: 1 HOUR
SERVES 6 - 8

4 Tblsp. butter
1 cup sugar
3 eggs, beaten
3 cups flour
2 tsp. baking powder
2 cups guava pulp
1/2 tsp. freshly grated nutmeg
1/2 tsp. cinnamon
1/4 tsp. ground cloves

Cream butter with sugar, add eggs; beat well. Add sifted flour and baking powder. The dough will be stiff. Roll the dough out to about 3/4 inch thickness with a rolling pin. Mix the guava pulp, nutmeg, cinnamon and cloves together and spread over the dough, leaving a margin around the edges. Moisten edges, roll up and seal the ends. Flour a pudding cloth and wrap around the Duff. Tie the ends, leaving room for Duff to swell. Place on top of a saucer in a saucepan of boiling water. Cover and boil 1 hour. *Slice and serve with Butter-Egg Sauce (see below) or Hard Sauce (see page 122).*

Butter-Egg Sauce

PREPARATION TIME: 15 MINUTES

1/4 lb butter
3/4 cup sugar
1 egg, separated

Cream butter and sugar, add egg yolk and blend. Beat the egg white until stiff and fold into the mixture. If too thick, add a couple of drops of hot water.

HARD SAUCE

PREPARATION TIME: 10 MINUTES
CHILLING TIME: 30 MINUTES
YIELD: 1 CUP

1/2 cup butter, softened
1 cup confectioners sugar
1 tsp. vanilla essence or 1 Tblsp. brandy

Cream butter; gradually add sugar. Continue beating until creamy. Stir in flavoring. Chill at least 30 minutes. *This sauce is wonderful served with Guava Duff and other puddings.*

GOOMBAY CAKE

PREPARATION TIME: 10 MINUTES
COOKING TIME: 1 HOUR
SERVES: 8 - 10

1/2 lb. butter
2 cups sugar
4 eggs, beaten
1 cup flour
1/2 cup pineapple soda drink
2 tsp. vanilla
1/2 cup shredded coconut
1/2 cup glacé cherries, halved

Preheat oven to 350°F. Grease and flour a large loaf pan. Spread cherries in pan. In a large bowl, cream together the butter and sugar. Mix eggs into the butter and sugar mixture a little at a time. Add flour and soda alternately with vanilla. Fold in the coconut. Pour batter into pan. Bake 1 hour.

Bahama Mama's Index, Glossary, and Conversions

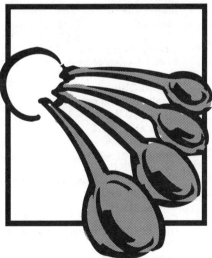

INDEX

(BY CATEGORY)

INDEX
(BY MAIN INGREDIENT)

GLOSSARY

Breadfruit: Also known as breadnut; a bumpy skinned fruit introduced to the Caribbean from Tahiti. Choose firm fruit with a yellowish green skin; flesh is pale yellow brown, starchy, soft and bland tasting.

Cassava: Also known as manioc, tapioca, yuca, Brazillian arrowroot; a tuberous root originally from Brazil. Choose large, elongated, oval shapes with dark brown skin. Contains poisonous prussic acid which is cooked off. Substitutes include potatoes, yams or eddo.

Eddo: Also known as taro, dasheen, coco; a tuberous root native to West Africa. Has a small central bulb with larger side tubers. Starchy taste similar to a potato. Make sure root has no blemishes.

Guava: Also known as a yellow guava; a native fruit to tropical America and the Caribbean. Small, roundish fruit with a greenish yellow skin with white, pink or very pink flesh. Contains many seeds which can be discarded.

Mango: Also known as "the fruit of paradise"; a native to South East Asia, brought to the Caribbean from Brazil. Usually yellow, orange or pink with small black or brown spots. Yellow orange flesh surrounds a large stone. Use a green mango as a vegetable.

Papaya: Also known as paw paw; a yellowish orange fruit. Green papaya is used as a vegetable. Choose fruit which is firm and unblemished.

Pigeon Peas: Also known as congo peas, gunga peas, gungo peas; a native of Africa. Peas from a perrenial bush with dark green brown pods.

Soursop: Also known as guanabana; a native to tropical America and the Caribbean. Usually heart shaped with a prickly green skin. The flesh is white and it contains several large, black seeds. Similar to the sweetstop and the custard apple.

Tamarind: Also known as tamarin; a tart and spicy brown pod used in Angostura Bitters and Worcestershire sauce. Use unripe tamarind for chutneys and curries.

MEASUREMENTS AND EQUIVALENTS

U.S.	Equivalent	Metric
Dash	Less than 1/8 teaspoon	
1 teaspoon	60 drops	5 ml.
1 Tablespoon	3 teaspoons	15 ml.
2 Tablespoons	1 fluid ounce	30 ml.
4 Tablespoons	1/4 cup	60 ml.
5-1/3 Tablespoons	1/3 cup	80 ml.
6 Tablespoons	3/8 cup	90 ml.
8 Tablespoons	1/2 cup	120 ml.
10-2/3 Tablespoons	2/3 cup	160 ml.
12 Tablespoons	3/4 cup	180 ml.
16 Tablespoons	1 cup or 8 fluid ounces	240 ml.
1 cup	1/2 pint or 8 fluid ounces	240 ml.
2 cups	1 pint	480 ml.
1 pint	16 ounces	480 ml. or 0.473 liter
1 quart	2 pints	960 ml. or 0.95 liter
2.1 pints	1.05 quarts or 0.26 gallon	1 liter
2 quarts	1/2 gallon	
4 quarts	1 gallon	3.8 liters

Weight

1 ounce	16 drams	28 grams
1 pound	16 ounces	454 grams
1 pound	2 cups liquid	
2.20 pounds		1 kilogram

TEMPERATURE CONVERSION

Fahrenheit to Celsius: Subtract 32, Multiply by 5, Divide by 9
Celsius to Fahrenheit: Multiply by 9, Divide by 5, Add 32

Fahrenheit	200	225	250	275	300	325	350
Celsius	93	106	121	135	149	163	176

Fahrenheit	375	400	425	450	475	500	550
Celsius	191	205	218	231	246	260	288

(These are rounded figures. *In cooking, use relative amounts of heat.*)

ORDER FORM

Qty	Title	Price	Total
	SHIP TO SHORE I	$16.95	
	SHIP TO SHORE II	$16.95	
	SIP TO SHORE	$12.95	
	SEA TO SHORE	$16.95	
	SWEET TO SHORE	$16.95	
	SLIM TO SHORE	$16.95	
	CARIBBEAN ADVENTURES	$12.95	
	BAHAMA MAMA'S COOKING	$12.95	
	STORE TO SHORE	$19.95	
	6.5% Tax (NC only)		
	Freight $3.00 per book		
	TOTAL		

Please charge my: ☐ Visa ☐ MasterCard
☐ Discover ☐ Amex
☐ Check ☐ Money order/ Payable to: Ship to Shore, Inc.
My credit card number is:

Exp. date

Autograph to: _____

Ship to: _____

Autograph to: _____

Ship to: _____

For orders
call toll free
1-800-338-6072
or use our website
www.SHIPTOSHOREINC.com
CapJan@aol.com

Mail to: Ship to Shore Inc., 10500 Mt. Holly Road, Charlotte, NC 28214

Signature_____ Date_____

✂ —

FREE

THE PERFECT GIFT
FOR ANY OCCASION

Share the Ship to Shore Cookbook Collection with your friends. We will send your friends a beautiful color brochure. Simply fill out and mail this form, call **1-800-338-6072**, email CapJan@aol.com or visit our website **www.SHIPTOSHOREINC.com**

Name _____

Address _____

City _____

State _____ Zip _____

Name _____

Address _____

City _____

State _____ Zip _____

Mail to: Ship to Shore Inc., 10500 Mt. Holly Road, Charlotte, NC 28214